DAY OF THE LIVING ME!

Adventures of a Subversive Cult Filmmaker from the Golden Age.
by Jeff Lieberman

Jacket art by Rick Trembles

To Vinnie
A real mensch!
xxx

For Cooks and Pooker

CONTENTS

Jeff Lieberman • Day Of The Living Me!

Adventures of a Subversive Cult Filmmaker from the Golden Age.

The year was 1953 and the Russians were about to drop the big one on us any second. True story! Google it. You couldn't watch a newscast or government sponsored public service announcement or television documentary without being reminded about our impending nuclear demise. And since no one believed the government would lie to us, Americans of all ages were bracing for complete annihilation. So when New York Governor Averell Harriman instructed every homeowner to build a bomb shelter in his or her basement, the terrified six year old me and my older brother Gary jumped right to the task. The civil defense department issued everyone a household booklet that focused only on the proverbial suburban family of four; specifically, the returning married veterans and their children who would later be referred to as "baby boomers." I suppose they figured those who lived in city apartment buildings would be at Ground Zero and wouldn't stand a chance, but we suburbanites might survive to build a new civilization, if only we could stay put in our bomb shelters until the radiation subsided in two hundred years.

Our tiny Long Island Cape Cod house had an unfinished basement which, according to the booklet, was ideal for a bomb shelter. My brother and I spent an entire afternoon crouched in the corner stacking sand bags exactly as illustrated in the booklet. Then came the supplies: canned goods, water, flashlights, battery-operated transistor radio, and every other necessity listed except for one. We decided to forego the bible. Even at that age we had already laughed off the concept of religion, agreeing with Albert Einstein that it was no more than a bunch of ancient superstitions. Fairy Tales for adults as Al put it.

Once we finished setting everything up it was back upstairs to our black and white rabbit-eared twelve-inch Zenith T.V. for the latest updates on when the Russians might attack.

Jeff Lieberman • Day Of The Living Me!

Our readiness was honed during school hours too with the "duck and cover" drills that could occur at any time during classes. While lecturing about, say, Columbus's trip to the new land, a teacher could suddenly blurt out the word "Duck!" This meant drop our pencils, scramble under our wooden desks and cover our heads with our hands. This government-mandated program never made the slightest bit of sense to us because it seemed to ignore their own propaganda documentaries which clearly spelled out that the A-bomb explosion approaches the heat of the sun which would not only quickly vaporize our wooden desks along with us, but the shock would reduce the whole school to rubble and the teacher's parking lot to a sheet of glass.

This government-induced anxiety laid the basis for many future billing hours of psychotherapy for us boomers. But in the meantime, a new kind of monster movie was being born that combined science and fiction to create "The Radiation movie." This was Hollywood's attempt at cashing in on all those well-laid fears.

My brother and I were drawn to them like moths to a flame. Nearly every Saturday it was off to the neighborhood movie theater for the monster movie matinee. Me, Gary and our gang of friends always got there early so we could get front row seats, never realizing at the time that those were actually the worst seats in the house.

The first radiation movie we saw was *The Beast from 20,000 Fathoms* about an atomic bomb explosion that awakens a pre-historic beast from the depths of the ocean. Pissed off for being so rudely awakened, the Tyrannosaurus-like monster comes ashore to terrorize the cities. Then all branches of the armed forces fight back and the beast is finally conquered - a huge relief for us after being scared shitless for over an hour.

Though I wasn't aware of it at the age of six, I now realize those radiation movies weren't only designed to cash in on the paranoia that had been instilled in us, but also to work as a catharsis with each story being a metaphor for the terrifying world around us. Whether the subject was a dinosaur-type monster, giant mutated ants like in the movie *Them*, or radioactive human transformations like in *The Day the World Ended*, the evil in each case was defeated. This gave us hope that since science caused these problems, science can solve them, either by figuring out how to kill the monster, or reversing the affects of radiation. This was very comforting and gave us hope for the future. Or rather, a hope that we'd actually live to *see* a future.

That is, until a movie came along in the summer of 1957 which broke

Adventures of a Subversive Cult Filmmaker from the Golden Age.

the mold and rocked my ten-year-old self's world like it was hit by an atomic bomb. The movie was called *The Incredible Shrinking Man*.

Directed by Jack Arnold and adapted for the screen by Richard Matheson from his own novel. The movie tells the story of average everyman Scott Carey (played by Grant Williams) who goes for a leisurely sail with his wife Louise. While she's below decks the boat passes through a mysterious low cloud hugging the water's surface, leaving a misty vapor on Scott's exposed chest. Director Arnold doesn't outright tell us this misty mass is the residual effect of an atomic bomb test, he uses spooky Theremin sci-fi music to say it for him.

Instead of growing a third eye and scales like the residual effects of exposure established in earlier radiation flicks, Scott's contamination caused him to shrink. Shrink! A concept, which absolutely horrified me because, like most other ten-year olds, I was obsessed with growing. I was looking forward to catching up to my brother and even my father some day. Now, here was a full-grown man like my father shrinking until he was shorter than I was. If not for the fact that I had two of my friends sitting beside me, I would've fled the theater right then and there. I looked down at my knees trying to avoid the horrors on the screen.

But then, all of a sudden, Scott Cary stopped shrinking, and my heartbeat slowed to normal. I laughed with relief, Ha ha, that wasn't so bad. So what if he's stuck being four feet tall for the rest of his life? Lots of grownups are four feet tall. Like jockeys, or circus midgets. Sure enough Scott did hook up with a circus performer who was actually shorter than him. She even needed to get up on her tippy toes to kiss him. Never expected this to end happily. I started slipping on my jacket while I waited for the words 'The End.'

But it wasn't the end, far from it. When Scott's new girlfriend tried to kiss him again, Director Arnold yanked the rug out from under us with a simple shot of Scott's shoes, punctuated by a spooky music sting, as he stood on his toes to reach her. Fuck! He was shrinking again!

CUT TO: Scott in a dollhouse. A freaking doll house! I froze. I couldn't swallow. From then on until the end of the movie I just sat mesmerized at what I'd later learn were called 'special effects' making it seem like Scott was at the same place as his giant cat, then later trapped in his basement with a giant spider, giant mousetraps, giant everything.

Scott's wife found bloodied clothes remnants of his encounter with their cat and assumed he was eaten alive.

When Scott screamed out to her, she couldn't hear him. He was too tiny to be heard by anyone. There'd be no rescue. No cure for the radiation induced hell Scott was trapped in. This was mortality. This was man's fate. He gazed at the night sky through the screened basement window.

"From my prison, a grey friendless area of space and time."

When Scott finally shrank small enough to step through the screen he pondered that the infinitesimal and the infinite were both the same thing and to God there is no zero.

"What was I?" he asked, "Was I still a human being? Or one of the men of the future?" Meaning that legions of others will be exposed to radiation from then on. Including me!

Death. Infinity. Two concepts I had avoided thinking about until then. And if science couldn't save Scott from the A-bomb, then I was doomed too. We all were.

I indentified so greatly with Scott Carey that I was convinced I was shrinking too. I associated the darkness of the space void he stepped into with the shrinking process, so I had to keep my lights on all night. Though I didn't observe any shrinking, I had to be sure so each morning I insisted my mother measure me against a chart she drew on the refrigerator.

As it turned out, I haven't to this day felt any effects of radiation, shrinking or otherwise. But those movies showed me what a powerful impact the horror and sci-fi genres can have not only in capitalizing on prevailing fears of the day but also in delivering political and social commentary from outside the boundaries of societal norms. The genre is also inherently subversive, which I am by nature, so I naturally gravitated to it when I first considered making movies myself. When I eventually moved on from the horror genre I continued to instill political and social commentary into my work, which wasn't the safest career path to follow, but at least it felt like mine.

Over the years that path zigzagged in unexpected and wonderous directions, resulting in interacting with a wide variety of iconic figures in the entertainment world and in the most unusual ways.

After a while I got in the habit of writing down these encounters in an on going journal while they were still fresh in my mind and a few years ago I started assembling them in chronological order, then worked them into an overall story narrative. I was surprised at how different each story was from each other, which really shined a light on the eclectic nature of my career. Along with all the stupid mistakes, hair brained schemes and disappointments, they also inadvertently revealed my creative process as it evolved, a detailed anatomy of a borderline whack job.

Adventures of a Subversive Cult Filmmaker from the Golden Age.

The result was a sort of career memoir. Not an autobiography, as my personal life outside of film is rarely discussed, but one big chronical of my oddball adventures in the film world.

Then I put it all aside feeling, okay, I did it, with no sense of urgency to do anything with it.

Until now.

At the age of 73 that childhood nightmare has returned... only this time it's real! I just had my yearly physical and while my doctor looked over my chart, he matter-of-factly pointed out that I've lost an inch in height since I've been seeing him. And since there's no scientific antidote for the geriatric shrinking process, I had to get this book out there before I shrunk into infinity like Scott Carey!

Childhood home, Valley Stream N.Y.

1. THE GENERATION GAP

1969 was a good place to start, as that seminal year they say defined the 60's. What it defined for me was one year out of film school and having no idea how in hell I could possibly make a living let alone have a career based on the little I learned at The School of Visual Arts. Basically a fine arts and advertising school at the time, the newly born SVA cinema studies program was still in the process of figuring out how to run a film school while we students basically stood by and watched. One good thing I got out of the school was finding out from Ernest Pintoff, my one semester screen-writing professor, that I possessed a talent for writing. The other good thing was meeting a new girlfriend, JoAnn Santoro.

JoAnn and I didn't get involved romantically until after we graduated but the chemistry between us was palpable from the start. After dating for a while I unofficially moved into JoAnn's rent-controlled, fifth-story, walk-up shit hole on the Upper East Side. It was one of those railroad flats; two tiny rooms separated by a galley kitchen. The whole place was crawling with high-energy cockroaches fueled by the restaurant below.

I needed to make some money to help chip in on the rent and after networking with my fellow SVA alums finally landed a short freelance job at a small company called Cannon Films. In those days Cannon specialized in re-cutting and dubbing Swedish soft-core movies into English for American consumption and their assembly line of edit rooms took up an entire floor.

Cannon's next soft core release was *Inga* starring Swedish bombshell Marie Liljahl. The original Swedish editor was Ingemar Ejve, but in order for the film to appeal to American audiences it needed to be dubbed and re-cut for pacing. The woman assigned to this job was known as a fixer. She was a pretty but hard-looking biker type named Mary Franklyn whose demeanor made it clear that her tight deadline gave her no time for chit-chat. It was my job to assist her, which mainly meant re-winding reels and retrieving edit trims from the bins. I couldn't believe I was getting paid to watch a nudie film. Okay, in short spurts, on a tiny screen. But still, it was a complete departure from my film school editing classes.

If there were no alternate shots that fit Mary's needs, like a rear shot of a woman riding 'cowboy style' during a very fake-looking fuck scene, Mary matter-of-factly instructed me to go through the outtakes of other Cannon Swedish releases to find a blonde fucking shot from the back angle. It didn't matter if the blonde was taller, shorter, fatter or skinnier as long as she was blonde.

Being a film school graduate, I couldn't believe the incompetence of this woman. You can't just throw in a shot of another person from another movie and pretend it's the same person the audience has been watching. But she was my boss so I went along with this useless exercise, found a blonde in a fuck scene and rolled it down until the camera was on her back, then handed it to Mary.

"She's blonde but no way is this gonna match," I said with the certainty of a cineaste. Without bothering to make eye contact let alone respond, Mary held her hand out and I gave her the clip. She quickly fed the film into the movieola and with a yellow grease pencil marked a cut point, then made the splice and fed the full scene back into the moviola while I stood by watching over her shoulder. When the new shot went by I didn't even notice it.

It worked perfectly, despite my SVA degree-enlightened knowledge. Then it dawned on me that this wasn't film school, this was the real professional world and I actually didn't know shit about making movies!

Suddenly this epiphany was interrupted by a man shouting down the hall outside. "The Niggers. The niggers are getting' all the money! Why the fuck work when you can screw and have babies and get paid for it? Welfare. They get all that welfare money. They even get free rubbers. Think they use them? Hell no, the only way they make money is makin' babies. They sell the rubbers then they use the money to buy booze!"

"Who the hell is that?" I asked Mary.

She took the grease pencil out of her mouth to say, "Some movie they're cutting across the hall," then marked the next shot.

At the first opportunity I meandered into the hall to see where this crazy guy's voice was coming from and it was booming from the edit room right across from us. "The social workers, how come they're all nigger lovers? You

7

find a social worker that ain't a nigger lover and I'll massage your ass!"

This didn't sound like any Swedish soft-core movie I ever heard. In fact it didn't sound like any movie I ever heard. The tall hippie-looking long haired editor caught a glimpse of me laughing and waved me in. He had a ready smile and was very enthusiastic about what he was working on.

"Listen to this one!"

He rolled the movieola and I watched a balding half drunk man at a bar spouting to anyone who'd listen. "All you gotta do is act black and the money rolls in. Set fire to the cities, burn a few buildings, throw a few bombs you get money and jobs. If you can't read you got a better chance of gettin' hired!"

We both cracked up. "What is this?" I asked.

"A movie called 'The Gap,' but I'm trying to get them to change the title." He shot out his hand to shake, "Bill Sachs."

"Jeff Lieberman. Who's that guy? He an actor?"

"Yep, Peter Boyle. Only good thing in the movie."

Bill went on to explain that this opus was Cannon's first attempt at legitimacy, a non soft-core outing they financed and produced themselves. Susan Sarandon made her debut in the movie as the 'hippie chick' whose father murders her drug dealer boyfriend. Helmed by a soft-core director-cameraman named John Avildsen, the finished product fell flat and didn't appeal to any particular target audience. The term 'Generation Gap' which 'The Gap' referred to was a media invention mocked by hippie baby boomers. The test screening went so badly people walked out in droves, so Cannon fired Avildsen and brought Bill in to somehow fix it.

Then Bill hit play and Joe continued his rant, "And the kids, the white kids. They're worse than the niggers. Money don't mean nottin' to them. Motorcycles, marijuana, five-dollar records. I got a kid, couldn't get into a regular college. Wanna know why?"

Then, with a gleam in his eye, Bill pulled another take from the edit bin, fed it though the sprockets and hit play. "Forty two percent of all liberals are queer!" shouted Joe. "That's a fact!"

We both cracked up. This guy was freaking hilarious. And Bill's instincts told him that if we were laughing, our entire generation would be laughing too, so he dug out every single piece of footage he could find and sculpted the movie around Peter Boyle's character 'Joe.' Even though Joe was just a supporting character in the original version, Bill's idea was to elevate this racist bigot to co-starring status.

Christopher Dewey, a descendant of Admiral George Dewey by the way,

Adventures of a Subversive Cult Filmmaker from the Golden Age.

and his partner in crime at Cannon, Dennis Friedland, loved Bill's approach to salvaging the movie and followed his lead by changing the title to 'Joe.' The movie caused an immediate tidal wave of publicity and in no time broke box office records for an independent low budget film, grossing nineteen million on a one hundred-thousand dollar budget. Screenwriter Norman Wexler was even nominated for an academy award and the movie put Cannon on the map as a legitimate small studio. There'd be no more soft-core releases from then on. In order to raise money for future productions, Cannon used this success to go public on the stock exchange. The following year, TV producer Norman Lear did an adaptation of the British series 'Til Death Do Us Part' and used the character of Joe as inspiration for the blue-collar everyman Archie Bunker played by Carroll O'Connor in the hit series 'All in the Family.' Though John Avildsen was fired after that dismal test screening of the movie in its original incarnation as The Gap, that fact was buried along the way and he received all the accolades that came with directing a cultural phenomenon. This, in fact paved the way for his being hired to direct what would become an even bigger phenomenon, *Rocky*, five years later.

I sure learned a lot about the real world of filmmaking in those two short weeks but when my job on Inga was finished I re-entered another aspect of that world: unemployment. I then made up my mind that there'd be no more freelancing. I needed to land a steady job with a steady paycheck.

Cannon Films release of *Joe*, 1970

2. FOOD FOR LOVE

It was spring of 1969. After about a month of begging I finally landed a hundred-dollar-a-week, entry level staff job at a New York City TV commercial production house called N. Lee Lacy and Associates located in a townhouse on 61st street between Lexington and Third avenues, a short block down from Joe Namath's infamous Bachelor's III. Though advertising had nothing to do with the 'cinema' that was emphasized by SVA, at least a TV commercial production company would be shooting film with professional cameras and lighting and since my short gig at Cannon convinced me I didn't know jack about film I figured maybe I'd even learn something in the process.

I quickly gained the confidence of the guys who ran the company and when their staff production manager was caught stealing, they promoted me to take over his job at three times my entry-level pay. Among my various responsibilities was putting together crews and I inevitably got chummy with many of the regular freelance hires. One of my favorites was a talented art director named Charlie Baxter. He was a tall, bearded Ichabod Crane-like hippie, about ten years my senior. Charlie was a member of that special breed who was able to light up a joint first thing in the A.M., chain-smoke joints all day and still function at a high level.

During breaks in shooting, or at lunch, Charlie would gorge himself with anything sweet to satisfy his near terminal munchies condition, and the added sugar high would shift him into a manic gear and a rap that usually involved some monumentally insane get-rich-quick idea. Like Ralph Kramden on speed, Charlie always had his eye on the prize of some elusive fantasy retirement in the south of France. I heard so many of Charlie's pitches I learned to stop questioning the validity of them because they'd just

Adventures of a Subversive Cult Filmmaker from the Golden Age.

be replaced by the next day's colossal idea. So when he approached me at the lunch table with, 'You gotta hear this man!' I scooted over to make a space for him and pretended I was all ears.

"Shoot."

"I'm going into the luxury yacht business!"

With that, Charlie unrolled professional-looking blue prints of an old, rusted out merchant vessel. "She's in mothballs now so I can get 'er for a song. Pump a few million into her and voila!"

Charlie flipped the page revealing his rendering of a magical conversion to a beautiful ocean going yacht. Very impressive indeed.

"Cool. So now all you need's a few million."

"I got it man! I mean good as got it. In three weeks I'll be rolling in the green!"

"What's in three weeks?"

"There's gonna be the biggest 'Be-In' in history, man! Up in Woodstock. Over a hundred thousand people! Maybe a million! It's gonna have music and art shows, and everything man! Gonna be called the 'Woodstock Music and Art Fair.' Dylan's gonna be there. Even the Beatles! And the Stones, you're into the Stones right? People coming from all over the country. They'll all be camping out for three days!"

Despite my routine skepticism of Charlie's schemes, this one peaked my curiosity. "What's this got to do with getting money for that yacht?"

"Plenty, man. All those people are gonna have to eat right? Who do you think has the sole food concession rights to feed them?"

Charlie's Cheshire cat grin said it all.

"What do you know about catering?"

"Absolutely nothing!"

Charlie slapped me five then broke into a stoner's coughing laugh, then lit up a roach remnant from his morning joint, rose from the table and went back to work. And I went back to eating lunch while the scheme Charlie just bent my ear with made its way out my other ear and up into the sky like a kite broken free of its string.

A week later I was on a sound stage immersed in the production of a huge Excedrin commercial and was helping mount diffusion parachutes over studio 10 K lights when I got a surprise visit from JoAnn. She couldn't wait to tell me about some big happening up in Woodstock featuring lots of big rock groups. She'd bought tickets for the two of us for the whole weekend and showed them to me excitedly, along with a newspaper ad for the festival.

11

Jeff Lieberman • Day Of The Living Me!

The tickets said, "Woodstock music and art fair" with a symbol of a white dove perched on the neck of a guitar. A cliché hippie dippy image if I ever saw one. But 'Woodstock' rang a bell. That's Charlie Baxter's dream number twenty-seven oh two! Holy shit, that's really happening? Goddamn, maybe his ship actually will come in this time.

I perused the line-up. No Beatles. No Stones. No Dylan. Richie Havens? You kidding? He used to show up from time to time at my Directing Actors class to make some extra cash. So did Joe Santos early in his career. Richie was a sweet fellow, always mild-mannered and upbeat. But he had no top teeth, which made it hard not to laugh when he was doing something like the Brando role from *On the Waterfront*. I never saw him sing but I could only imagine what he sounded like without those upstairs choppers. None of the rest of the line-up thrilled me either. Arlo Guthrie? Please. Hendrix? Never liked him. Sure he was a consummate guitar player, but I was never into what they were calling 'acid rock.' Joe Cocker. Joe who? Janis I'd already seen in NYC a few times so no big deal there either.

Had JoAnn been a guy, just some buddy with two tickets to this thing, there's no way I'd go, even with my Charlie Baxter connection. However, JoAnn was not a guy. She was my new smoking-hot, Catholic-schooled, innocent Italian girlfriend and no way was I letting her venture up into the woods alone to camp among hordes of free-loving, stoned-out hippies for two nights.

"This is gonna be really cool!" I lied, and then scooped a parachute from the un-used lighting pile.

"We can use a couple of these silks to make a tent. Just string them between some trees. And we don't have to bring food because my art director Charlie Baxter has all the food concessions!" She giddily threw her arms around me and we sealed it with a kiss.

The following Thursday we set out at the crack of dawn in my beat up powder blue 1964 Sunbeam Alpine two-seater sports car. We figured we'd get there a day early and beat Friday's traffic.

My tiny car had just enough room in the trunk for the parachutes and our change of clothes. I wedged a wooden tent pole between our seats along with a bag of Oreo cookies I bought at the last minute to sustain us until we got to the festival and hooked up with Charlie.

When we reached the New York State thruway headed north, it soon became clear that a lot of people got the same idea as us, and by the time we turned off the exit headed to Route 17, we were met by heavy traffic of early-bird vehicles of every description from Volkswagen buses to campers,

Adventures of a Subversive Cult Filmmaker from the Golden Age.

family station wagons, you name it, all moving at a snail's pace with the festival site still at least twenty miles away. After about a half hour, all traffic came to a complete halt. A half hour after that, it was clear we weren't going anywhere and one by one people started shutting their engines, so I finally threw in the towel and shut mine too.

A chorus of crickets and cicadas instantly replaced the engine noise. The humid late summer air was thick with the smell of fresh honeysuckle. Swarms of mosquitoes, which are always up for some new blood, started chowing down on us from every direction. We pulled up the convertible top and latched it tight, then rolled up the windows. This stopped the mosquitoes, but quickly turned the car into a sauna because the black cloth roof started baking in the sun.

Up to that point, most of the girls I'd dated were "JAPs." Though it stands for Jewish American Princess, I learned through experience you don't have to be Jewish to be a JAP. And everyone I'd dated would already be complaining about the stifling heat, the cramped quarters of my tiny car and the fact that it had no air conditioning and smelled musty with the top up. But JoAnn just sat there in silence as the temperature rose and the sweat poured down both our faces. I didn't know her well enough to know what to make of it. Was it a slow burn? Was she about to explode?

Finally she turned and just looked at me and we spontaneously started laughing. At the situation. At everything. Then she said, "Where're those Oreos?" I plucked the bag from between the seats and we both tore in. Nothing we could do but just sit there munching, waiting for the cars ahead of us to miraculously start moving again.

Hours later it was clear we weren't going anywhere so we tried to hunker down and get some sleep, which was nearly impossible in those tiny non-reclining bucket seats and a stick shift poking up between us. Add to that a steady stream of people bumping into my car as they passed, having decided to abandon ship and hoof it from there.

The Friday morning sunrise re-ignited the steamy heat and when I pulled down the top, first thing we noticed was that most of the cars around us were abandoned and pretty much everyone had committed to hiking the rest of the way which was many miles. It looked like a scene from The Ten Commandments with thousands carrying their belongings and trekking ahead to the horizon and beyond. My car was too easy to break into to leave it there so I made a snap decision, twisted the key and turned over the engine.

"I'm turning around."

"To go home?"

"No, circling back to the Thruway..."

I couldn't believe the only way in or out of an area the size of the festival grounds was this one main road. There had to be another way to get there so off we went.

Even though I was now a man with a plan, it was still a strange feeling driving at fifty miles per hour in the opposite lane headed east back to the thruway and away from this history-in-the-making event. That's a lot of hard fought, stop-and-go driving to give up in a matter of minutes. And worse, it looked like we were bailing out to all those hundreds of cars we were passing. Seemed to them we had enough of the nineteen sixties dream and were headed back to the city like a couple of cowardly straights. They jeered and booed us all the way back to the thruway where the northbound lanes were backed up looking south for as far as you could see. But heading north from where we were was clear sailing; there wasn't a car on the road but ours. My plan was to take the next thruway exit, which turned out to be Route 52, circle west over the highway, then zigzag diagonally on country roads on a hypotenuse route back to the festival.

After turning off the main route, the roads were mostly unpaved and certainly not suited for little British sports cars. For the next hour we wove, skidded and splashed through deep gouged out puddles, sometimes winding in the exact opposite direction I wanted to go but doggedly zeroing in on my imagined destination point. Finally we ran out of roads altogether. All we could see were endless miles of cow pastures and cornfields. Our journey seemed to be over. We were both starving and in need of water too. But the thought of doubling back, not only to the thruway, but all the way back to Manhattan, was so objectionable that the situation called for desperate measures. Since the roof was already down on the car, I asked JoAnn to get out and hold up a barbed wire fence that kept the cows in the pastures, and trespassers like us out.

I ducked my head down as low as I could, put her in first gear and made it under the wire without being decapitated. Once on the other side of the fence it became instantly apparent that beneath the lush green grass was this gooey black mud that covered the wheels as they spun around, with gears grinding and engine revving to the red line.

JoAnn got behind the car and pushed and the black mud shooting out of the wheels spewed all over her, making her look like Al Jolson in drag. When I finally gained traction, JoAnn hopped in and off we went, slip

Adventures of a Subversive Cult Filmmaker from the Golden Age.

sliding away through the first of a series of cow pastures. Most of them had old rusting 'No Trespassing' signs, pocked with bullet holes for credibility. I kept glancing toward a nearby farmhouse where I could just hear the owner saying, "Ma, we got some damn hippies on the property, go fetch me up the twelve gauge!"

Cows rarely look up from their business of grazing, but the sight of a powder blue sports car bouncing by, tent pole clanging, gears grinding elicited a chorus of 'moos', which sure as hell sounded like laughter, while their big round eyes followed us until we disappeared into the distance toward the Promised Land.

After weaving and skidding through half a dozen more farms, repeating the barbed wire lifting technique with each new trespass, we finally bounded onto a gravely road.

And then we saw it. It was like a mirage, right up ahead of us, a virtual sea of tents and camping vehicles, punctuated by the faint sounds of distant drums. I felt triumphant already. My hair-brained scheme had already paid off since we were now way closer to the festival than where we gave up what amounted to a parking space on Route 17.

I drove up as close to the main gate as I could, then dropped JoAnn off, instructing her to wait right there until I found a place to park. She got out and took her bag with her which contained the tickets, leaned in to kiss me, then strode off into the crowd. I turned the car around and after about a quarter mile, spotted a place to park in the weeds. I pulled the top back up, then yanked the parachutes from the trunk. But the only way I could carry both chutes, our change of clothes, sheets, pillows and the poles, was to devise a rig, tying each parachute into a sack on either end of the longest pole, stuffing all that stuff inside them, then straddling the pole across the back of my neck *Thief of Baghdad* style.

One of the many signature images of Michael Wadley's Woodstock documentary was the constant stream of open pick-up trucks rambling along that very same Road to Mecca, all piled high with hippies flashing peace signs and big friendly smiles. Next time you watch the movie, see if you can spot me, a pathetic figure trudging alongside them like Gunga Din. I couldn't, but I only saw the movie once.

I finally made it back to the front entrance and about five minutes later I located JoAnn who had to pee in the worst way but didn't want to miss me so she'd been holding it in. She took out the tickets and we ventured inside but there was nobody official looking enough to approach with our tickets and it seemed everyone else was just streaming in over the bent down flimsy fences without showing any tickets at all.

Now it was my turn to wait as JoAnn fell in place on one of the dozens of "Porto-san" lines. These portable potties already smelled pretty randy, even this early in the game. After what seemed like forever JoAnn emerged from her Porto-San holding her nose, then she let go and sucked in a lung full of fresh air, or rather, debatably fresher air. We entered the grounds and the giant stage was blocking our view until we got past it and saw that now famous "Sea of humanity" for the first time. We had another way of describing it, which we said in unison.

"Holyyyy shit!"

Rather than attempt to navigate through all those people, we set out for higher ground along the periphery. We figured the higher up we went, the better view we'd have of the stage, and we needed trees for my imagined tent construction anyway.

The music had already started and sure enough, there was Richie Havens up there on stage with a guitar, pounding away on it like it was a bongo drum while shouting to the heavens 'Freedom! Freedom!' He sounded soulful and convincing but it was pretty clear he still had no top teeth. (It was revealed years later that he used his Woodstock earnings for a new set of upper choppers.)

When we reached the high country that too was packed with people. So the decision became, who do you want to be your neighbor? It was like choosing the right spot to set down your towel at a crowded beach, only for a two and a half day stay.

Not everyone at Woodstock was all about peace and love. There were also hundreds of biker types, the sort who wanted to make war, not love, so choosing the right spot took some time.

We finally found a clear spot surrounded by tents adorned with colorful flags and symbols of unknown origin. It had a real hippie commune type vibe. Without further ado we settled down and I commenced construction. I used the real tents all around me as inspiration for what I was trying to achieve architecturally, while also trying to seem like I knew what I was doing. After some trial and error I got it all rigged to a nearby tree. With the pole propping up the center and with a makeshift doorway, my creation almost passed for a tent. A white nylon tent fit for a Sheik!

Now to find Charlie Baxter and get a Sheik's banquet going. JoAnn hung back tidying up the nest, while I, the hunter-gatherer, set out to do some serious gathering.

The sun had set and the glow of the fires were taking over as a primary light source, just bright enough for me to spot a sign that read 'Food For Love' with a hand painted arrow pointing straight ahead. Food for love. Perfect. Here I was a manly man putting food on the table for my love. It may have been that very moment I realized I was falling for JoAnn.

But as I closed in on Food for Love, I saw a spot light from a helicopter hovering overhead, with someone on a loud speaker announcing that the whole festival was being declared a disaster area. As I proceeded, I had to wade between a steady stream of hippies going the opposite direction, all clearly angry about something. I grabbed the closest guy's arm.

"What's goin' on?"

"All the food's gone and what's left's crawling with maggots man. We're a disaster area, they're calling in the National Guard to watch us all starve! Got any weed?"

Charlie and his culinary associates at Food for Love didn't arrange for refrigeration so the majority of the perishables had perished in the hot August heat long before the gates even opened. And just like that, Charlie's Luxury yacht took its place on the ocean floor alongside all his other pipe dreams.

By the time I found my way back to our camp, JoAnn had made up the inside of the tent just so, a perfect nest for us with all our clothes neatly folded and stacked to one side and a flat rock placed in the center to serve as our dinner table where she was seated on the floor by candlelight, munching on an Oreo. I rushed in and snatched the bag from her hands.

"We need to ration these! It's all we have!"

"Where's all the food?'

A loud silence was all I could muster.

"You find Charlie?"

"He fucked up big time and all the food's gone or contaminated."

To add insult to injury, I suddenly felt a drop of water on my cheek. Then another one. It was raining. But how can I feel it from inside a tent?

The drips started getting steadier and I held the candle up to the roof, which of course is the center of a parachute, which of course is wide open so the air can flow through during a jump. And so can water. Add to that the fact that the whole silk parachute itself is porous so air can pass through and five minutes later the rain was soaking through the tent as if it wasn't even there. JoAnn scrambled for our change of clothes, trying to bunch them up to keep them dry. But we were drenched by now, and so were our blankets, and there was no reason to stand inside anymore so we just got out and stood there in semi shock. No food. No shelter. No dry clothes. Of course this was entirely my fault. We could've brought a real tent like everyone else instead of relying on my hair-brained idea. And knowing that Charlie himself admitted to knowing nothing about catering, yet relying on him for food was equally foolish. Some hunter-gatherer I turned out to be. If our species relied on males like me, we would've been extinct eons ago. If I were JoAnn I would've called it quits right there.

But instead she pulled the cookie bag from her purse and exclaimed, "At least the Oreos are dry!"

"Oreos?!" came a voice from the darkness. "I'd give anything for an Oreo right now!" A few stoners emerged from the shelter of their tents and gathered around to gawk in awe at the sight of the familiar Nabisco cellophane bag clutched in JoAnn's hands.

Just the mention of the word 'Oreos' had aroused the most basic primal human munchies urge that's been part of man's existence since he emerged from the syrupy swamp and discovered ganja. One stoned out Hippie chick neighbor couldn't contain herself.

"Man, I'd ball both of you for an Oreo!"

Then a few others nearby got in on the bidding until one guy said, "Dig this man... I'll give you half of this hero for one of those."

"Deal."

He handed over his salami and provolone sandwich in exchange for an Oreo and immediately shoved the cookie in his mouth. I tore a piece of the sandwich off for JoAnn then wolfed down the rest. Not bad I told the guy between bites.

"My mother made it. I've got more in the cooler. But it'll cost you a few more of those."

Then another freaky looking guy chimed in. "How bout a joint for one of those cookies man?"

I did a quick inventory of the cookie bag. We had two full lines of Oreos left. In the brave new world of the Woodstock festival this meant we were rich! JoAnn and I, two tiny specks in that legendary 'sea of humanity,' could very well be the only ones holding a half bag of slightly soggy but still very edible Oreos. Four hundred and fifty thousand stoned-out hippies, all suffering from advance cases of the munchies and craving anything sweet, anything chocolatey, and we were holding the goods!

The word quickly spread and more people emerged from the darkness like zombies from Night of the Living Dead. For the next hour we bartered cookies in exchange for all the food, drink and pot we could consume. The homemade cuisine was beyond anything Charlie Baxter could've offered us even if he had known what the hell he was doing.

As dawn arrived, the rain had stopped. We sat there in the mud, cuddled up with a semi dry blanket wrapped around us. Soggy but content, we lived to see another day. JoAnn snuggled up closer and said, "Good thing you brought those Oreos."

"Yep," I said in a confident tone as if I anticipated all this, being one the great hunter-gatherers of our time.

You may be asking, what about the music? I don't really remember much. Like I said earlier, I wasn't really into any of the performers so it was the event itself, the spectacle of it all that stands out to me some 50 years later. The mother of all be-ins.

Back in New York City, for the year, JoAnn's tiny roach infested fifth floor walk-up remained our campsite. At least it was dry. By this point I'd worked my way up to directing commercials at Lacy. In fact, this was actually the first time I got to direct anything, even if it was just an advertisement for bed sheets. I never did see Charlie again since the festival, and while I was fairly certain he wasn't sailing the seven seas, I just hoped he didn't wind up in jail. Or worse.

JoAnn and I decided to get married, but we had no real plans beyond that. The money I was making, though no great shakes in the scheme of things, was already more than most of my friends were making at the time, and with little overhead I was able to periodically spring on impulse buys;

Mostly stupid shit like a pair of genuine rattlesnake skin boots. I had seen my idol Keith Richards wearing them and read that he got them at the Chelsea Cobbler in London. When they opened up a branch in New York, I grabbed a pair, which cost me around one week's pay. I nearly broke my ankle the first time I wore them, since I wasn't really used to walking on high Cuban style heels, but at least I hobbled along proudly.

Our Woodstock tickets, 1969

19

3. ADVERTISE THIS

It was pretty clear that my future was secure in a career making TV commercials. At 22 years of age I started directing commercials for Lee Lacy so all I had to do was keep doing it and I'd certainly be a player in that industry in say ten years time and be rolling in doe-ray-me. But my problem was, I didn't believe in reincarnation, meaning you only have one life to live and I knew that wasn't the one I wanted. So when a friend of mine from School of Visual Arts called me to produce and direct a commercial without the need of the company I was working for nor its high overhead I was all ears. His name was Marc Rubin and he worked for a hot new agency called Jerry Della Famina and Partners on Madison Avenue. Marc said they needed a commercial for a new beverage called Sportade, which was trying to compete with successful launch of Gatorade, and they needed it like yesterday, or they were in danger of losing the account.

"And you don't care if I do it for Lacy or not?"

"Nope, long as you can get it done fast."

That night I told my father about my plans and he called his lawyer who said I needed to incorporate myself for liability and tax purposes. I needed a name so the lawyer could set up the corporation. A name? I had no intention of making this an actual business, just a one off, so it didn't really matter what it was called. I was working for Lee Lacy and Associates and I never could figure out who his associates were but it did sound official so why not go with that.

So the next day I was president of Jeff Lieberman and Associates.

The Sportade commercial featured Mets catcher Jerry Grote and his son. Since the amazing Mets had miraculously won the World Series in the

Adventures of a Subversive Cult Filmmaker from the Golden Age.

fall of '69, the team was enormously popular and every player was cashing in on their newfound fame, even the catcher. The shoot was to take place in Mets spring training camp in St. Petersburg Florida. Bad luck would have it that an air traffic controller strike was called and there was no way to book a flight to Florida from New York. Rubin's agency was desperate and he told me to do whatever it took to get us down there so I got prices on private jets, finally negotiating a deal with Butler Aviation for a ten man job that would accommodate me, Rubin, and my film crew. The agency got the client to foot the bill for the overage so it didn't cost me a dime. The rental was for exactly twenty-four hours use. When we arrived at LaGuardia they ushered us to the tarmac and we stood by waiting for passengers of the previous flight to deplane. And low and behold the passengers were The Monkees, arriving in NY for a concert gig.

The flight down to St. Pete was harrowing to say the least because the pilot wouldn't give me a straight answer when I asked him how he could fly without radar or air traffic control. He kept putting me on about recognizing signposts, like mountains, lakes and even shopping malls. This banter had one of my crewmembers genuflecting in fear and another reciting the Hebrew prayer for the dead.

When we arrived at St. Petersburg airport our plane stayed put in a designated area on the tarmac, waiting to return to New York the next day. This put a lot of pressure on me because according to Murphy's law every filmmaker had to memorize, that 'anything that can go wrong will go wrong so prepare for it.' But preparation was not in the cards so everything had to go exactly right for me to pull this off which was asking an awful lot.

When we arrived at the training camp I was met by Jerry Grote and his representative along with Jerry's little boy. They were both dressed in Mets uniforms and the commercial was to show Jerry working up a sweat catching a game, pitch after pitch tight on him, then pull back to reveal it's just his son pitching the ball to him in a game of catch in an empty stadium. Then they both gulp down their bottles of Sportade. Simple right? Not to Mr. Murphy because the entire Mets team was practicing on the field that day! I pretended I had permission to shoot there and feigned surprise about all the players on the field to Jerry and his rep. My crew was not so sure and starting to believe they endured that harrowing flight for nothing. All I needed for the payoff shot was for left field to be vacant, but that was exactly where the team was doing their daily stretches and calisthenics. I knew I had only one shot at what I was about to do so I'd better make it good. I took a deep breath, then casually walked out onto the field, passing the great Brooklyn Dodgers legend Gil Hodges who was the Mets manager. I nodded a hello as if I was there on official business, then searched around for a groundskeeper and finally found one lugging a hose out onto the field. With as much fake authority as I could muster I told him that I'm shooting a little thing with Jerry Grote and his kid and wondered if he could possibly get the team to move over to right field for their exercises. For added incentive I pulled a couple of hundred dollar bills from the top of my pants pocket and flashed him a peek.

He took a moment to think of an idea on how to justify doing that. Since he planned on turning on the left field sprinklers after they were finished anyway, he could just tell them he needs to do it now.

"That'd be great! Thanks!"

I slipped him the Benjamins in a handshake then moved fast setting up the shot with Jerry and his son. In the distance, I watched the entire team get up off the grass and shift over to right field to continue their workouts, and in no time the left field sprinklers all went on. This made for a much better payoff shot of Jerry's kid because it sold the fact that they were using the stadium when it was empty, along with the Florida sun streaking through the misty outfield air for a great visual effect.

Back in New York I went straight into editing. But then it occurred to me that I was operating without an office. My sudden absence from Lacy was bad enough, I couldn't just conduct outside business from my desk there. I had to provide the agency with an official New York City (212) number for Jeff Lieberman and Associates so my only option was to pick a phone booth they could call. It had to be at a very lightly or never used location, not out on the streets of midtown where the traffic noise would easily give it away. I finally found the perfect booth just outside the Central Park Zoo cafeteria. It was a really nasty affair, stunk of urine and garbage, covered with graffiti and the door only half closed. But at least the phone worked and it was relatively quiet except for the birds. So from then on that was my outside office. One day when my editor had the thirty-second spot all cut and I was to discuss a scheduled payment with the agency, I arranged for a call at 2pm 'at my office.' I arrived at the phone booth five minutes early and to my horror, a wino was passed out cold on the floor of the booth, vomit on his shirt, sprawled half inside with his legs stretched outside. The phone started ringing. This was before answering machines so if it kept on ringing the agency would know there's no 'associates' in my so-called office headquarters. Since there was no waking the poor guy up I had no choice

Adventures of a Subversive Cult Filmmaker from the Golden Age.

but to yank the door open as wide as I could, then hold my breath as I stepped inside straddling him and finally reached for the receiver. About to turn blue I let out a lung full of air and with a gasp of air said;

"Jeff Lieberman and Associates."

"Mr. Lieberman please."

"Speaking!"

When I returned to Lacy and my old job, my boss was less than thrilled that I took an outside freelance job in direct competion to Lacy and while on their payroll to boot. They were right to be angry, and it just showed how little I cared about a career in advertising. In fact it showed me that I was probably just looking for an excuse to get fired. But the more my boss ranted, the more it became clear to me I wasn't being fired because he wouldn't have bothered lecturing me if I was. In fact, what I did probably frustrated him more than anything. The fact that I could be so brazen meant he didn't really have the kind of fear hold over me that he held over the other employees.

Shooting a commercial at Mets spring training camp, 1970

4. A MADE JEW

One day out of the blue came a call from Ernest Pintoff, my screenwriting teacher from film school, asking if I'd be interested in getting involved in a movie he was about to direct starring Red Buttons. Ernie already had a script but wasn't too thrilled with it and thought I could help 'punch it up,' whatever that meant. He said it'd be an ongoing process, re-writing as new cast members were hired and locations were chosen so I'd have to quit my job at Lacy to pull it off. Though every one of my fellow film students would've given anything to be directing commercials at twenty-three years of age, it was an easy decision for me to hand in my notice. No more selling cornflakes for me.

The movie was called *Who Killed Mary Whats'ername*, and low and behold the producers were Cannon Films, the company that made *Joe*. *Joe's* huge success enabled the partners at Cannon, Chris Dewey and Dennis Friedland, to raise a war chest of Wall Street money to make higher budget, more mainstream movies. *Who Killed Mary Whats'ername* would be their second step toward legitimacy and a chance to show that *Joe* wasn't just a one-off fluke.

Red Buttons was cast to play the role of Mickey Isador, a diabetic ex-prize fighter who takes an interest in solving the murder of a prostitute named Mary in New York's Hell's Kitchen because nobody else, including the police, seem to give a damn about her. Hence the title. Up to that point I had no actual screenwriting experience so it was "earn while you learn" time for me. Problem was, there was no line item in the movie budget to pay for another writer and I couldn't afford to learn for free.

The line producer of *Who Killed Mary Whats' Er Name* was a fellow

Adventures of a Subversive Cult Filmmaker from the Golden Age.

named George Manasse, a no-nonsense, nuts-and-bolts pro whom I knew from my stint in commercials at N. Lee Lacy. Ernie instructed George to get me on the movie in some capacity so George put me on the payroll under the budget line item location scout. But the brass at Cannon understood that unofficially I was also to serve as resident script doctor.

I thought the location scout title was just a ruse to justify my paycheck, but George knew from my commercial experience that I was fully capable of performing that role and known for what John Waters famously coined 'making a dollar holler.' George's plan was that after the locations were all set I would then be designated as location manager so I'd get paid throughout the entire production.

This scheme delighted Ernie, as it would allow me to focus on the re-write, but George explained to him that nailing down locations had to be the first priority in order to set all the other production elements in motion.

So off I trekked to Hell's Kitchen, the mythical setting of 'West Side Story.' By now it was late February, freezing cold, and I was this twenty-three-year-old kid emerging from the Eighth Avenue subway in my snazzy snakeskin boots, which were already starting to molt.

As I crossed over 10th Avenue, much to my chagrin, those old fire-escaped tenements where Tony romanced Maria were overshadowed by new skyscrapers. Most of the immigrant candy stores, luncheonettes and bars were gone; only a few remained. Shooting them while hiding the behemoths all around would be impossible. Every camera angle would betray the old mixed in with the new.

There was only one other place I could think of in the city that might still capture the insular immigrant neighborhood vibe the script called for and that was to center the entire production in Little Italy. So it was back on the subway for a ride downtown.

As I emerged from the Canal street station it became clear that if there was ever a fish out of water, I was it. I immediately drew suspicious looks as I stood at the corner with no idea which direction to turn. The West Village was my only downtown stomping ground, anything further south was foreign territory, so I just picked a random block and forged northward into Little Italy.

When you're scouting locations, you look at a place much differently than you would if you were just passing through, or as a tourist, or even a life-long resident. You look at everything in terms of the movie. You observe how locations fit in with the script, logistics of where the trucks can park, the noise levels and traffic at various hours of the day. And among the most important elements, especially in an insular old neighborhood like this is to be welcomed by the locals. This was a skill I excelled at during my stint in commercials. I somehow managed to make it all sound so glamorous and exciting to have twenty or so sweaty guys trekking through your house for a Post Toast'ems commercial. I figured feature films shouldn't be much different. In fact, this should be even easier because a real movie connotes celebrity and glamour and money. Me being part of it would probably make me sort of a celebrity to them also. Yeah, that's right I thought, I was now part of Hollywood!

I re-adjusted my dark Ray-bans, pulled out my location list and sauntered into a small luncheonette, which the script called for. Inside, I looked around and it was absolutely perfect. The commercial business conditioned me not to allow my enthusiasm to show. Act nonchalant. Much like when buying a house, letting on how much you like it only strengthens the seller's bargaining position. I casually approached a man at the register who I assumed was the owner.

"Hi, I'm Jeff Lieberman. My company is just in the preliminary stages - but there's a small possibility your place might fit for our movie ..."

"No movie! We cloz-ah! I go home now!" He rushed around the counter, grabbed my elbow and ushered me out the door. Then he flipped the "opened" sign to "closed."

Jeez, I thought. He must've had people shoot there before and had a bad experience. Oh well, on to the next one. But to my surprise, I got a very similar reaction at the next restaurant, and the one after that. As soon as I said the word 'movie' the conversation was over. What the hell was going on?

After another hour of this, my ankles were killing me because those boots were not made for walkin'. I had to get off my feet before I buckled onto the sidewalk so I turned into the nearest bar at 129 Mulberry Street, corner of Hester. The name over the front door said Larry's Bar. It was a very run down old school joint, the kind of place only locals would frequent for that bare bones, cheap bar booze, solitary, barfly experience. First thing that hit me was the familiar pungent mixture of cigarette smoke, stale beer and questionable restroom hygiene that permeated most low-end NYC bars and bowling alleys at that time. As I slid onto a stool, I assumed the older weathered; wiry guy coming over to serve me was the place's namesake, Larry.

"Frank" he corrected me, "what can I get ya?"

I wasn't a drinker at all at that time, and none of my friends were either. This was all happening in the very thick of the recreational drug era, and alcohol, in all its forms, was rarely even mentioned in my circle. So in situations like this when I was actually just paying for warm stool rental, I'd order a beer from the tap with a plan to sip it until I was rested enough, and thawed out enough to forge on. Since I was the only customer, Frank wanted conversation.

"We don't get many hippie types in here. Don't get me wrong, your money's green as anyone's."

I took the hint and pulled out a dollar bill, then figured I might as well take one last shot.

"I was hoping you were Larry, the owner. I need a bar for a movie I'm working on. This would be perfect."

"What, *The Godfather*? Good luck with that." Frank reached over to a crumpled issue of the Daily news left by a previous customer and slapped it down in front of me. There it was, front-page story laying it all out, and explaining the cold reception I was getting.

The filming of Mario Puzzo's novel *The Godfather* was front page news because the Italian-American Civil rights league, founded by mafia boss Joe Colombo, didn't approve of the way Italian Americans were being portrayed in the screenplay and had a particular problem with the use of the word 'Mafia,' an institution Colombo insisted didn't exist. So the Don put the word out on the street, specifically in little Italy where much of the movie would take place that nobody should cooperate with 'the movie people' associated with *The Godfather*. There were already rumors of intimidation and death threats, and a confirmed report of a producer's assistant's car window being shot out.

So naturally when the immigrant generation in this mostly Italian neighborhood heard the word 'movie,' they instantly assumed I was referring to production of *The Godfather*. The machinations of Hollywood, which allowed for two entirely unrelated movie productions to shoot in the same general area, were simply not on their radar.

I closed the paper and handed it back to Frank. "But this isn't *The Godfather*. It's called *Who Killed Mary Whats'ername*. Stars Red Buttons."

"Red Buh-ins!? I love Red Buh-ins! You know 'im?"

"Yeah I know him," I lied, figuring I would eventually know him if I didn't get fired first for coming up empty on locations. And if that happened, I'd never have to prove to Frank that I knew him because I'd never see him again. So it was one of those rare, no-risk lies you get to tell over the course of a lifetime.

"An he'd be here?"

"Yeah, we need to shoot lots of stuff, a lot of it in a bar and this is perfect so he'd be right here, maybe where I'm sitting right now. Silvia Miles would be here too. So would Ron Cary..."

"Listen, no offense, you sure this ain't *The Godfather* cause holy jeez..." He pointed to the newspaper headline.

"That's exactly the problem I'm having. All I'm getting is 'no movie, no movie' and that's it. At least you let me explain."

Frank sized me up and started hitting me with a lot of questions to make triple sure I wasn't bullshitting, which eventually led to not-so-subtly probing into my personal life. "So, where you live? Where you from? Lieberman, Jewish name."

Instead of telling him to go fuck himself like I normally would whenever the Jew thing reared its ugly head, I had too much at stake here so I just nodded, then told him something that might help make me kosher in his world.

"Engaged to an Italian girl. Catholic school in fact."

"No shit!"

Frank's entire demeanor changed as he rushed to refresh my beer.

"So Red Buh-ins eh? Nothin' to do with *The Godfather*. A different movie that just takes place here."

I took another mini sip of beer, mostly foam.

"Just a murder mystery. Nothing to do with Italians or the mafia."

Frank could see I didn't want any more beer, so he took my glass and emptied it. "Go take a walk, feed the pigeons, they're starving this time of year." He reached under the bar and produced a bag of bar mix, a salty assortment of pretzels, nuts and crackers. "It ain't bird seed but they don't give a shit. Them things'll eat anything. Come back around four and meet Joe. He should be around then."

"Who's Joe?"

"Joe Carlo."

"He the owner? Then who's Larry? Larry's bar?"

"Just come back at four."

So I wandered around the neighborhood like a tourist, nibbling away at the bag of bar mix, flipping some to the occasional pigeon when I passed one. A kid from Long Island taking in the heart of Little Italy for the first time was not a welcome sight for the locals. In fact, no outsiders were welcome in this neighborhood until the natives were convinced otherwise.

I returned to Larry's Bar at four o'clock sharp. When I arrived, Joe Carlo was already there. Even though it was February in New York, the first thing

Adventures of a Subversive Cult Filmmaker from the Golden Age.

I noticed about him was his deep dark tan, then his tailored suit and sleek haircut. Though he was on the short side to begin with, the much taller and bigger men surrounding him didn't do his stature any favors. Frank did the intros, "This is Matty, meet Jeff, Joe, Jeff," after which I was led to a tiny back room with a table and checkered tablecloth. As we all sat down Frank brought each of us a small glass of anisette.

I was all ready to give Joe the pitch of how I'm not affiliated with *The Godfather* and how much I'd love to use his bar for our movie, and how we're fully insured, but none of that seemed to matter. Frank already said good for me or Joe wouldn't be talking to me so he just raised his glass and the others followed suit.

"Salud!"

I forced myself to swallow down what to me tasted like melted licorice and I hate licorice in any form.

"So, Frank tells me you're marrying an Italian girl?"

"Yep, that's true."

"Don't you lay a hand on her."

I looked at him and the others and they didn't seem to think there was anything wrong with that moronic out of nowhere warning.

"What? You're the guys who beat up your women, not us. That's why they call your tee-shirts 'wife beaters.'"

Joe's expression freeze-framed. So did the others. Instant dead silence. I really didn't think I said anything wrong, just a comeback to his stupid statement, the way I learned to survive in my blue-collar neighborhood on Long Island.

Suddenly Joe pointed his finger right at me while he barked to the others, "He's right! He's fuckin' right!"

Then Matty spoke up, "Ay, speak for yourself!

Joe poked at my shoulder.

"I like this kid. He's got some fuckin' balls!"

Everyone had a good laugh accusing each other of spousal or girlfriend abuse as Matty signaled to Frank for another round. Then Joe spun his finger around the inside of his emptied glass, licked it, then turned his focus on the business at hand.

"So, what? You wanna shoot a movie in here with Red Buh-ins? Okay, done. What else?"

I looked at him blankly.

"What else you need?"

"Oh, the other locations?!"

I yanked out my location list and handed it to him. Joe pulled down his half frame reading glasses and scanned the page while I pushed another document across the table.

"I also need you to sign this location agreement so we can shoot here. Six days and nights. The fees are right on there."

Joe made a face and pushed it right back.

"I don't sign. Here's how I sign."

With that he reached out and shook my hand, just as Frank arrived with the new round. "Drink up and we'll go take a walk."

I forced down the second shot along with the others, then we all headed out into the freezing air. As we walked east on Hester, it seemed like all the locals were clearing the way for us. Really strange, more than just being polite.

When we reached the next corner, Joe stopped and gazed at my location list. "Okay, who's got a freight elevator?"

"Ferrara's," said Matty, then pointed the way for me with a tilt of his head.

We entered the famous bakery through a back door that led to the kitchen and walked through without anyone even looking up from his or her work, while Joe made an announcement.

"This is Jeff, he's with the movie people. He might wanna shoot a scene in the elevator with Red Buh-ins."

One of the bakery chefs looked up and nodded, then went back to work. The elevator turned out to be perfect, great camera angles in every direction. As we left Joe called out again.

"Okay, Jeff's gonna be back with the movie people. He'll call you." Another casual nod and we were out the door. Joe and Matty pulled their collars up against the late afternoon icy wind. I did the same as Joe glanced down at the list again. "Okay, what else?"

With absolutely no resistance from landlords, storeowners or anyone, I was able to check off most of the locations I needed for the movie. A scout that was shaping up to be a disaster wound up being a total home run. If we could use Larry's bar as the central location at the corner of Hester and Mulberry, all the other locations were within blocks of that point. It would be almost like turning a small portion of Little Italy into a Hollywood backlot. Usually when something is too good to be true it is, but this felt like one of those rare exceptions.

Adventures of a Subversive Cult Filmmaker from the Golden Age.

When I got back to Cannon films and reported the news to George, the producer, at first I was an instant hero. In just one day, I'd landed most of the locations we needed and now the producers could plan out the actual shooting schedule. As happy and relieved Ernie was to hear it, he was very anxious to get me back on the script re-write and ushered me to his little office at Cannon to get to work.

No sooner than I started writing, George interrupted us, asking me for the location clearance papers. When I told him all I had was a handshake from a guy who only claims to own one of the locations, and nothing in writing on any of the others things went south fast.

George did a slow burn while he reminded me that this was Cannon's first 'legitimate' movie. Red Buttons was a big name star. The supporting cast by then consisted of Sam Waterston, Alice Playton, David Doyle and Conrad Bain, all important New York actors at the time. And it was a New York union production to boot. There's insurance issues and parking permit issues. You can't bank all of that just on a handshake!

I stressed emphatically that a handshake is the most we'll ever get and if I went back to push for signed papers it was a sure bet that Joe and company would just tell me to fuck off. Add to that the problem of *The Godfather* boycott encompassing all of Little Italy and trusting Joe's word looked like our only shot. As crazy as it sounded, George had no choice but to go along with it. Now the pressure was all on me to deliver.

By early April, Larry's bar was turned into our central movie set where Red Buttons' character, ex-fighter Mickey Isador, would drop in to get information from the bartender played by Ron Carry. To save money on signage we kept the name Larry's bar for the location, which I inserted into the working script while also re-naming Carry's character Larry.

Joe and Matty were around every day for the shoots, loving every minute of it. At the end of the first day I joined Joe out on the sidewalk and handed him an envelope containing six one hundred-dollar bills. He checked the contents then looked at me.

"What's this?"

"Location fee for one day shooting at the bar. What we agreed to…"

Oh shit, I thought. This was it, the moment I dreaded was coming. He waited until we were fully invested in shooting at his locations, with trucks and cameras and lighting and trailers and permits and all that goes into a location production in New York city, then suddenly pretend we didn't have any agreement on anything and nothing in writing to prove otherwise. In short, was this going to turn into a monumental shakedown all because of my faith in this one guy? Joe cracked a cold smile, reached into his pocket and pulled out a stack of betting tickets from Aqueduct racetrack.

"See this?"

He pulled a rubber band away and started flipping tickets on the sidewalk. They were all 50 to 100 dollar tickets. Then Joe shook his head and said, "That's around five grand I lost today. What am I gonna do with six hundred?"

Oh boy, I thought, here comes the shakedown and it's gonna be huge. I'm fucked. We're all fucked. I braced myself as Joe stepped out to the curb and pointed around the area.

"Take that money and hand it out to the neighborhood. Give them little errands, like get coffee, move some cars, like they're workin' on the movie."

"Got it," I nodded, completely hiding my relief. "What about tomorrow's fee, and all the other places?"

Joe waved his hand around. "Same thing. Spread it around, put 'em all to work." Then he yelled out to a man setting flowers out in front of his grocery store. "Ay Rico! This is Jeff. Tell everybody to help him out with things to do. He'll take care of ya." Rico nodded and went about his business, just like those pastry workers did in Ferrara's.

My father had been taking me to the race track since I was ten, so I was very familiar with horse betting which really impressed Joe. Not nearly as much as being engaged to an Italian girl, but enough to get him into a conversation about horses, which led to him telling me that he owned a few ponies himself. In fact, he had one running that Saturday so maybe I wanted to come around the Big A. "If you do, look around the clubhouse. We're around."

I called my dad from the phone booth in the back of Larry's and it turned out he was planning on going to the track that day also, so Saturday afternoon I joined him at his usual seats in the clubhouse. Seated right nearby were the usual regulars, the great Cab Calloway, the actor Tom Ewell and Phil Silver's older brother.

I got up to go place a bet for my dad and on my way back I ran right into Joe, Matty and a very tall guy named Frankie who did not possess a discernable neck and seemed to be wearing thick shoulder pads. Matty reached out to shake my hand.

"Ay, Jeff, good to see ya! Who you like?"

"Going with the two."

Adventures of a Subversive Cult Filmmaker from the Golden Age.

Matty laughed out loud to Joe.

"Uh oh, that's a jinx. Bettin' against us."

"No, never. Didn't know you have a horse in this race."

Joe held up some win ticket bets.

"The six. But you might've done right with the two. We'll see what happens."

Then Joe pointed down and said, "Meet ya back here after the race."

I returned to my seat and looked down at the paddock area and sure enough, there was Joe, giving a jockey a leg up onto the number six horse. My father pointed out that Joe's horse was trained by Joe Campo who was notorious for his connections with the mob and training their horses.

Then he stated flatly. "Be careful with these people. They want something from you."

The mob? As in the mafia? That organization that Joe Colombo insisted didn't exist? Makes perfect sense. That's why they were able to waltz into Ferrara's and all those other places like they owned the joints. Maybe they really did!

Joe's horse ran up the track and our two horse finished third. My dad ceremonially tore up the tickets and we both flipped the paper to the next race. When we arrived at our next pick, I got up and headed to the windows and as I approached, I saw big Frankie literally running across the clubhouse's shiny linoleum floors. When he spotted me, he skidded to a halt and then came over panting for air.

"Where was ya?"

"Down in the boxes sitting with my father."

Frankie pointed to the exact tile Joe pointed to before the race. "When you wasn't there after the race like you said, Joe got worried something happened. I'll go tell him you're alright."

Now, when most people say something like they'll 'meet you back here after the race' they mean at some point. It could be right after, or a half hour later, or even two races later depending on how things go. And "here" certainly doesn't mean that exact linoleum square on the clubhouse floor Joe was pointing to. But to these guys it did. And in their world, the only acceptable reason for not being there right after the race was if I was kidnapped… or worse.

"Tell Joe I'm sorry. I got all wrapped up in figuring the next race." This gave me a glimpse of another side of Joe and his friends. A darker side. And with the knowledge imparted by my father, I stood there wondering, why were mob guys bringing me into their world? And treating me so nice? Was my father right, that they wanted something from me? What could they possibly want from me?

As the production proceeded, first George and Ernie, then pretty much every department head relied on me more and more to make last minute miracles happen on the set. Things like moving parked cars that were blocking a shot, last minute access to apartments to get great camera angles and most importantly, a neighborhood that would never complain to the police when we went hours overtime. Gradually they all got greedier and took my special relationship for granted, as if it was part of the every day production plan. And with each new favor, I felt my debt to the mob increased. So I started bullshitting them about how Joe was getting annoyed by all the things I kept asking him for and that from then on they should figure out another way to get things done.

Meantime, Joe Columbo and his Italian American defamation league finally made peace with Paramount Pictures and now *The Godfather* was shooting in Little Italy at the same time we were. Sometimes just around the corner.

One particular afternoon word got out that Marlon Brando would be filming a scene just a block away from us on Mott street, and that he was gonna get gunned down right on the sidewalk! So during our lunch break a bunch of our crewmembers went over to kibitz with their fellow union brothers working on *The Godfather* just to get a close up view of the shooting scene. Sounded good to me, so I tagged along.

Mott Street was all dressed to look like it did in the 1940s with old cars, period signage, prop vegetable carts and extras in period costumes. We all stood along the curb and watched as the Godfather picked out veggies while his oldest son Fredo sat in a black sedan waiting. Coppola yelled 'action' and two thugs pumped nine rounds into *The Godfather*'s back sending him to the pavement along with a variety of produce.

Coppola yelled "Cut!" then rushed in to congratulate Brando on a convincing performance. Sure looked realistic to me, and movie scenes like that generally don't when you're watching from only thirty feet away.

After a few cleanup shots of Fredo sobbing over his father's lifeless body, it was a wrap for that location and a big white school bus pulled up. Brando waved to the locals then followed his fellow cast members inside the bus. Someone on his crew must've alerted him that a bunch of crewmembers from another movie were watching across the street because the bus suddenly made a sweeping U-turn and as it passed us, Brando stuck his naked ass out the window and mooned us! Not a pleasant site but funny as hell.

Next day, *The Godfather* publicity machine was in full swing. All the daily papers covered the story with production photos of Brando being gunned down, but none of them captured the moon shot. I sure wish we had cell phones back then. The papers also reported that while Brando was getting shot down on Mott Street, Carlo Gambino, one of New York's real godfathers, was sitting right around the corner in a Grand Street cafe, "sipping black coffee from a glass and holding eighteenth-century court in twentieth-century New York."

Like it or not I was in the epicenter of organized crime and actually "in with the boys" myself to some extent. The favors done for our production amounted to untold thousands of dollars we'd have spent if we had to make the movie without their help. But it became increasingly clear to everyone that Joe was doing the favors for me, not the production. And as the favor tab piled up, all I could think of was my father's warning. What the hell could they possibly want in return?

The day of reckoning came soon enough. Frank the bartender said Joe wanted to talk to me about something. Uh-oh, I thought, this is it. Would he ask me to pull a robbery? Move stolen goods? Worst case, kill someone? He had to know by looking at me I was no tough guy. But maybe that's what he was looking for, someone who could go undercover without being suspected! My mind whirled with possibilities and none of them ended well for me.

Joe was waiting for me at the back table of Larry's and the anisette was already poured. It was just Joe and me this time which in a way made it even scarier.

"Jeff, sit down. Salud!"

We drank. "So Jeff, I need to ask a favor."

My heart started pounding so hard I could hear my own pulse. "Sure. Anything."

"When Sophia Loren shot a movie down here, her husband Carlo Ponti did us the honor of hosting them for dinner at La Luna." He twisted around and pointed to the famed Italian restaurant further down on Mulberry. "Could you arrange to do me and Matty the honor of taking Red Buh-ins and Sylvia Miles to La Luna? With you and the Director of course."

"When?"

"Saturday night."

"Done. I'll make a reservation."

"Nah, none of that. We won't have a problem."

Joe shook my hand excitedly, then patted me on the back.

"So when's the wedding?"

"Not nailed down yet."

My mind was reeling. Could that be it? I was driving myself crazy for nothing all that time? I slid into the phone booth and called Red at his hotel. Fortunately I caught him in his room.

"Jeffie boychick! What's shakin' my favorite Yiddel?"

"I need you to join us at La Luna Saturday night."

"Ah, I can't. Got some people comin' in from the coast."

"Actually it's important. Sylvia too. And Ernie and I will be there."

"Sounds like fun but I'll take a rain check."

"No rain checks. I told our hosts you'd be there."

"Oh, how considerate. Who's so important you didn't check with me first?"

"Joe Carlo, the owner of Larry's. And his friend Matty."

"Ho ho! That figures. Mob guys always like to be seen with movie stars. Even the ancient ones."

"Mob guys? Why do you think that?"

"You kiddin'? I knew first time I laid eyes on them. I used to know Joe Bonanno. Went to parties at his house and entertained the troops."

"Okay, so?"

"Think I want my legs broken? La Luna Saturday, what time?"

"I'll swing by the hotel at seven and pick you up."

And that was it, all set. Joe and Matty would get to show off to their friends at La Luna, and my debt to them would be paid. Or so I thought.

When the movie was finished Frank gave me a telephone number to call if I ever needed anything. He said Joe wanted me to have it which gave it special weight and implication now that I was starting to get the picture of who his circle of friends were. As I was about to leave Larry's bar, which would be for the last time, Frank added, "Oh, I forgot. Joe wants to know where you're gonna live."

"What?"

"After the wedding. You need a nice place. There's this new complex the city's building. Downtown. Right on the water. They call it low-income but that's bullshit, they don't check. Two-bedroom for what you're payin' now for that shit hole."

Adventures of a Subversive Cult Filmmaker from the Golden Age.

"Sounds great. I'll look into it."

"Forget about it. There's over a thousand names on the waiting list. So Joe wants to know when you could move in."

"But what about the list?"

"That's the thing. If you wanna move in in six months? You'll be what, number a hundred? If you wanna move in next week you'll be number one. He just gotta know."

This sounded so strange to me I didn't know how to react, so I just thanked him and said I'd speak to JoAnn about it then call and let him know.

JoAnn was dead set against it. "That sounds illegal. We could get into a lot of trouble. And also, you'd owe them even more for it." She also didn't like the idea of me carrying that telephone number around. "What are you gonna use it for, have someone killed?"

I must admit the thought had occurred to me. Someone starts giving me shit at a bar, two guys, ten guys, doesn't matter. "Ay, see this dime? I make one fucking phone call and you're all dead!" Now that's something someone wearing cool high-heeled snakeskin boots would say.

To keep the peace I promised I wouldn't take Joe up on his offer, even though I had no idea where our next campsite would be after the wedding. One thing was clear, we weren't raising a family in a one bedroom, fifth-floor, roach infested walk-up railroad flat.

Canon Films informed me that they couldn't give me a shared credit since script rewrites were not officially contracted in a writer's category. But to show their appreciation for the contribution I made they gave me an Associate Producer credit, which was my first official movie credit.

On April eighth a year later, I picked up the morning paper and the headline read, "Gangster 'Crazy Joe' Gallo gunned down in Little Italy restaurant." Perusing through the story the mob hit occurred at a place called Umberto's clam house. Strange that I never even heard of it, having spent so much time down there. The next sentence got my full attention; the place was located at 129 Mulberry Street on the corner of Mulberry and Hester. That's the exact address of Larry's bar!

Turned out Umberto's opened in February '72, eight months after we wrapped the movie. I bought up all the other New York papers and here's what the reporters said about the people I nearly became seriously involved with.

Joe's real name was Joe "Joe Carlo" Calabro. He was sort of the Genovese family's public relations man and the untitled mayor of Little Italy.

Jeff Lieberman • Day Of The Living Me!

With the Chinese buying up blocks of real estate, Joe worked hard to keep Little Italy Italian. He was also a close associate and friend of notorious mobster Mateo Ianniello, aka "Matty the Horse," the same big Matty who was always around watching us shoot. The same Matty who was at the track. The same jovial Matty who joined us at La Luna!

It was right around that time that Matty Ianninello was promoted to capo régime of the Genovese crime family. It was claimed that Matty controlled over 80 restaurants and sex-oriented clubs in New York, including most of those located in the Times Square area of Manhattan but also other bars and nightclubs throughout the city. Clubs like the Peppermint Lounge and most of the gay bars like the Stonewall in the village were all owned or controlled by Matty. The mob loved these unlicensed clubs because the gay crowd were known for drinking twice as much of the mob's watered-down alcohol than straights and more importantly had a voracious appetite for all the various illegal drugs the mafia pushed all over the city. Later on in 1995 when Genovese boss Vincent 'The chin' Gigante went to prison, Matty would be made acting boss of the family. Who knows, maybe if I'd stuck around with those guys I would've been a made Jew by now called "Jeff the Snake" (after my boots.) Or, more probably, Jeff the dead. Matty also owned the building at 129 Mulberry under his brother Robert's name which included Larry's bar on the ground floor. Soon after we wrapped the movie, Robert converted the bar into a restaurant, and supposedly laundering some of Matty's money into a legit business called Umberto's Clam House. But just two months after the opening of Umbertos, "Crazy Joe" Gallo dropped in for a late birthday dinner and was gunned down by members of the Colombo family. Matty was in the kitchen that night but swore he didn't know anything about the hit.

The Godfather had been released and suddenly everyone was talking about the Italian mafia, the exact opposite result to what the sanctimonious Colombo claimed he wanted. It all hit me in a rush, this bunch of nice guy wise guys I'd been hanging out with were, at least according to the Feds, actual bigtime gangsters who temporarily took me in as one of their own.

When I relayed all this information to JoAnn it confirmed her worst fears and she let me have it good. She might not have been a JAP but she sure was Italian and for the first time I got to see that side of her as she threw a plate across the kitchen. I feared for my life, more than I ever had with Joe and his cronies. "We could've been in that restaurant with your stupid gavone friends, you jerk!"

Adventures of a Subversive Cult Filmmaker from the Golden Age.

She was right. Had I stayed in touch with my wise guy friends, I surely would've known all about the Larry's bar conversion to Umberto's and I could just hear Frank telling me that Joe and Matty wanted the honor of treating me and my Italian fiancé to dinner there. Maybe even on the night Joey Gallo got whacked!

But JoAnn wasn't finished yet. "Where's that number they gave you? Tear it up. Right now or I'm not marrying you!" I was just as freaked as she was and couldn't flush it down the toilet fast enough!

My cameo appearance in *Who Killed Mary What's 'Er Name.*

Cover art of VHS release of *Who Killed Mary What's 'Er Name.* A young Sam Waterston in lower right corner.

5. MARSHALL MCLUHAN, WHAT ARE YA DOIN?

With the movie behind us, Ernie asked me write a new feature film with him. Seeing what I could do on the fly on *Mary Whats'ername*, Ernie thought we should take a crack at writing something together from scratch.

He already had an idea in mind. To explain it, he first had to explain the genesis of his idea, which also included how in hell he could afford to live in his fancy high-rise on Madison Avenue. I always did wonder about that so I was all ears.

As Ernie told it, while straphanging on the steamy summer subway headed downtown to see his divorce lawyer, Ernie glanced down at a pulp paperback setting on a woman's lap, then found himself reading the description on the back cover. "…Detective Frank Clancy, a loose cannon rogue cop, needs to keep a key witness alive for twenty-four hours so he can testify at his mob boss brother's trial. The mob wants him dead…"

When the woman turned the book over, it revealed the title. *Mute Witness*, which hit the plot line dead-on.

Ernie thought that simple story line would make a good movie, only he was so broke from the divorce, he had to get his friend, producer Phil DiAntoni, to front the five hundred for the option. The plan was that he and Phil would produce it together and Ernie would direct.

Ernie was very into Marshall McLuhan's new concepts of understanding contemporary media and in 'McLuhanese,' the title 'Mute Witness,' just didn't cut it for a movie. It was okay for a book but too 'hot' for the 'cool' medium of movies. So Ernie changed the lead character of the book from 'Lieutenant Frank Clancy' to Lieutenant Frank Bullitt, just so he could call the movie itself *Bullitt.* He knew that when you said it out loud, it sounded exactly like "bullet," but also it implied action and violence while the different spelling made it almost justifiable as a cop's legitimate surname.

The idea of changing the spelling would also solidify it as a trademark, which was even cooler. Now, some 40 years later, simple applications of McLuhan's concepts have become the norm in pop culture. Think one-word brand singers like Cher, Madonna, Sting, Prince, Rihanna. Movie titles like *Jaws*, *Alien*, *Saw* or a movie that happened to be in theaters at that time called *Shaft.* "John Shaft. Can ya dig it?"

Ernie didn't write *Bullitt.* His divorce lawyer, Alan Trussman, did. He didn't direct it either; Steve McQueen accepted the role on the condition that Peter Yates would be at the helm. Pissed off by the slight, Ernie withdrew from the production altogether, leaving Phil DiAntoni to produce it himself.

By controlling the property, Ernie maintained his producer's deal as if he'd gone on with the production, which included back end royalties from what turned out to be a big hit for Warner Brothers. Hence, the expensive apartment, which triggered fantasies of making a score like that myself. "So, what's this got to do with *Bullitt?*"

"*Blade.*"

"Blade?"

"Tommy Blade."

"Who?"

"Bullitt?"

"Yeah?"

"Blade.' Detective Tommy Blade. Tuff. Street. New York. Smokes cigars. Low budget. Hand held. All on New York locations."

Ah, I got it. He wanted to sort of rip-off the *Bullitt* concept with another cool, one word cop title. "Okay. What's the story?"

He didn't have one. He didn't think it was really all that important in the post 'Blow-up' new world of cinema. Story was secondary. If you wanted to be cool like Antonioni or Bergman, you couldn't let story get in your way. The important thing was the look, the style, the feel; the existential gestalt of it all. And along with Marshall McLuhan, Ernie was going through a serious Costa Garvas *cinema verite* period at the time too, which he first experimented with in making *Mary Whats'ername.'* Only this time he wanted to go all out gorilla, John Cassavetes-style.

The plan was we write the script together, produce it together and Ernie directs. So this time I was assured to be credited as co-writer of the screenplay. We knocked out Blade in a very short time because we were writing directly to a formula (or what would later become a formula) the rogue cop movie with dialogue like, "What happened to you Blade? You used to be the best there is." Since neither of us was ever arrested and our only direct interplay with the police was to ask for directions, our corny stilted dialogue was drawn mostly from a combination of movies and TV series.

When we finished off the script, Ernie tried to raise financing from a variety of sources, each time dropping the budget to fit a new player. By the time it got to Don Rugoff, head of the Rugoff theater chain, it was rock bottom no budget so Rugoff agreed to bankroll the whole thing.

But at that budget level, there was barely any money for either of us. Ernie could afford to do it all on spec but for me it'd be a big sacrifice to work for nothing and wait for a payoff that may never come. The fact was, I didn't believe it'd ever come because I didn't really believe in this concoction and such a low budget meant there'd be no stunning car chases or spectacular explosions to bail out the movie.

So, I declined to work for nothing. Ernie took it as a betrayal and I guess in retrospect maybe he was right. Either way it damaged our relationship from then on.

Ernie made the movie anyway casting John Marley in the lead role of Tommy Blade. In yet another link to *The Godfather*, Marley was just coming off his legendary characterization of studio boss "Jack Woltz." The young, then virtually unknown Morgan Freeman even bagged a small role in *Blade*. Not invited to any screenings, I finally got to see the movie in a drive-in down in Deerfield Beach, Florida. There it was, 'written by Ernest Pintoff and Jeff Lieberman' right up there on the big screen. My first official writing credit. The movie was tough and gritty all right. You could barely see the night scenes but it was *cinema verite* all the way.

Blade bombed at the few venues it played in, not even earning a small fraction of what *Bullitt* did, which somewhat validated my decision to drop out, even if Ernie never really forgave me.

6. THE RINGER

I landed a meeting for a possible professional Directing job at King Features Syndicate located on 45th Street a couple of blocks up from Grand Central Station. King is a division of the massive Hearst Corporation and that encompassed their library of cartoon characters who appeared both in the Hearst paper's comic strips and cartoon shorts in movie theaters and TV. Among them were Popeye, Flash Gordon, Blondie, Beetle Bailey and Ripley's Believe It or Not.

But this job opening was in their "school reel" division, which cranked out those educational public service and news films projected by nerdy AV squads in classrooms across the country. Major sponsors lined up for this public service exposure, which made it a very lucrative business, and King was among the biggest distributors.

I hadn't directed anything to show as an example of my work, but I did have production experience on my resume and my young age and appearance probably were factors because anyone with long bushy hair that looks like it could nest a pterodactyl and wears what was left of those snakeskin boots must be in tune with what the kids are thinking. They weren't entirely wrong.

My meeting was with a man named Jerry Berger, an attorney and Vice President of King Features, who explained the assignment to me. It was to make an anti-drug film for public schools across the country that wouldn't be dismissed and laughed at by the new generation of young people.

By the late 1960s to early 70s the government propaganda division had been at it again. Instead of nuclear war, this time it was about the evils of drugs. Only the illegal kind of course. But young people were a lot more media savvy by then and had caught on to their game. This time they weren't scaring anybody. In fact there was nothing more fun than getting high and watching those "this is your brain on drugs" public service commercials, or throwing erasers at classroom screens showing inane, tedious so-called anti-drug films.

That was the problem King and their new sponsor Pepsi Cola was facing. They wanted to take a different approach, do something the kids could relate to instead of laugh at. Berger told me to go home and think about it and we set another meeting for the following week.

So I thought about it. Anti drugs? First of all, I was never anti drugs. I'd never be stupid enough to stick a needle in my vein, nor challenge the power opiate narcotics had in creating human addiction, so heroin and speed were off my menu. So was LSD because I did it once and it scared the hell out of me. To this day I'm not entirely sure I ever fully came down from it. But cannabis in all its forms came very naturally to me. It fit my personality in some mysterious way. It clarified what was already swirling around in my head, helping me distill it all into ideas and concepts.

So, fully aware of the irony, I lit up a joint and focused in on the assignment, to make an anti drug film the kids can relate to. Okay, since I wasn't anti drugs in general, if I try to fake it and claim I was I'll wind up with the same pandering crap they're trying to avoid. So I took another tack and asked myself, what am I anti? What do I feel strongly against that impacts the youth culture and might overlap into this general subject? The answer was that I was anti marketing, especially marketing products to susceptible young people using media manipulation techniques. Okay, I was on to something. Like what products? Music is one. Clothes and fads is another. And drugs? Are drugs being marketed to young people? Damn right they were! Only the marketing was being done by the kids themselves! I grabbed my yellow pad and wrote down the words "peer pressure." Then I thought about the false claims and the hip lingo that went with the whole drug scene like "very fine stuff" or "this stuff is outrageous." If I could illustrate how the music and fashion businesses manipulated young minds to sell their products and then make a direct parallel to how drug dealers were doing the exact same thing to sell theirs, maybe the kids would take notice. Nobody wants to be manipulated, no matter what their age.

I tried to come up with some fad item that back in 1971 nobody would believe any kid would ever go for. Something extreme to illustrate how you can sell anything to kids if you market it right. I wrote that line too, which of

Adventures of a Subversive Cult Filmmaker from the Golden Age.

course would be coming from an advertising executive. The item I came up with was a nose ring. And a campaign for an item called *"The Ringer,"* a kit of various shaped nose rings and how to get the kids to believe they thought of this fad themselves. I'd then show how a new rock group is marketed in a similar way, getting the kids to buy into the pre-packaged image of the group. This would make a natural transition to drug dealers at the top and then tracking their wares down to the street level, all using the same sales lingo to push what they're selling. The result would be a group of kids in a suburban home listening to that rock group that was marketed to them and trying on nose rings while they waited for the drugs they swallowed to kick in. I called the movie itself *The Ringer.*

When I returned to King Features the following week and pitched my idea, Jerry Berger listened but really had no idea what I was talking about. But it was very clear it was nothing at all like the run of the mill antidrug films that were failing so miserably. He found my enthusiasm for my idea more encouraging than the content of my pitch because it meant if I connected with it with such passion, maybe the kids would too.

He gave me a green light with the proviso that it be done on a rock bottom budget. I guess he was covering himself for a complete disaster that King would have to eat because Pepsi's money only came into play from the purchase of prints for the schools. So to keep the budget on a shoe string, I'd have to shoot as much of the movie as possible at King's corporate offices on 45th street. I was also limited to casting the lowest rungs on the acting ladder, people who would work for next to nothing. I had to use the Hearst news crew as my film crew, a group that never shot anything scripted in their lives. My first attempt at directing would be with no Director of Photography, no Assistant Director, no Script Supervisor, pretty much no anything. All I had was a field cameraman, his news crew and a 16mm Ariflex news rig, a bunch of portable lights, and a soundman.

One of the actors I selected was a guy named David Groh who went on to play Rhoda's husband in the hit series *Rhoda* and another was Charlie McGregor who was fresh out of prison. Charlie later landed a role in *The French Connection* and also played Freddie in the hit movie *Super Fly*, the Freddie of the song "Freddie's dead" sung by Curtis Mayfield.

The resulting twenty-two minute 16mm short, *The Ringer*, was test marketed to various high schools across the country. The reports came back with mixed results. Nobody threw their pencils at the screen; in fact the kids were riveted by the film up until the ending. But then the Pepsi logo came on and they booed and hissed and probably tossed a few projectiles, which ironically meant they got the message of the film all too well because that Pepsi logo stood for a company selling brown dyed, sugar-filled carbonated water for a hundred times what it cost to make by target-marketing their swill to a new "Pepsi generation." When these results got back to Pepsi they not only dropped out of their sponsorship of the film, they fired the executive who made the deal with King Features.

Crap. It looked like my first attempt at writing and directing a movie was a complete failure and without sponsorship wouldn't be seen by anyone other than my family and friends. I started second-guessing myself. Maybe I should've done something more conventional. Which made me wonder if Blade's conventional story and dialogue wasn't so off the mark after all. I never had to take outside opinions into account and maybe playing it safe by emulating what's been done before was the key to commercial success in the film business. Even though King Features specifically told me that the conventional anti-drug films weren't working and that Pepsi wanted something different, the reality was that something different wasn't what they wanted either.

So when I got a call at my parents' house from the president of King Features himself, a man named Milt Kaplan, I assumed he had gotten the news of Pepsi's withdrawal and would be demanding I return my meager fee for making the movie. I braced myself for what was coming while he informed me he'd seen the movie. Then he said he was more proud of it than anything King had ever done and that I had a home at the company as long as he was running it. With Kaplan's endorsement the film was entered into a slew of major film festivals which included the Chicago, Atlanta and Cine-International festivals and it won the top prize in the public service category at every one of them. Off that exposure, the Xerox Corporation, who was not burdened by a marketing scam image like Pepsi was, took over sponsorship and the film went on to be a big money maker for King Features and Hearst.

Had someone told me that twenty years later teens in shopping malls would be wearing an assortment of rings in their noses I would've asked that person what drugs they were on.

7. STAR WARS IN MY EYES

From then on I was King Features' wild-haired boy and Jerry Berger, with all of the award trophies *The Ringer* won proudly displayed on his desk, encouraged me to develop any of the properties they owned I saw potential in. Those iconic titles, which as I mentioned before included *Popeye*, *Blondie, Beetle Baily, Ripley's Believe it or Not* and *Flash Gordon*.

Over the next year I fooled around with each of them, which helped keep me afloat financially. I even made a *Popeye* safety film, with Popeye instructing little school kids on how to cross the street without being reduced to roadkill. During post-production I got to work with the great Jack Mercer who was the actual voice of Popeye and also voiced Felix the Cat. Jack made his entrance into the recording studio literally cursing like a sailor in perfect 'Popeyeze!' He had us all laughing so hysterically it was near impossible to get the narration track done. Wish I'd kept a copy of his X-rated version of the narration I wrote.

The one King Features property I saw the most potential in updating was *Flash Gordon*. While going through the comic artwork for *Flash Gordon* and then screening the old 1930's Buster Crabb episodic serials, I imagined what it would look like if it was a new movie. I, like practically everyone of my generation had recently had their minds blown by Stanley Kubrick's *2001: a Space Odyssey* and I flashed on an image that combined Kubrick's vision of 'real' space age technology with the fantasy action and larger than life characters of *Flash Gordon*. Here's how I pitched it to Jerry Berger:

"It looks like *2001* with the same computers and scientific technology, only with robots shooting ray guns over the computers like cowboys in a western!"

Jeff Lieberman • Day Of The Living Me!

Jerry smiled, nodded, then told me someone else was in his office pitching him the same thing while I was making *The Ringer*. "A fellow named George Lucas." I'd never heard the name.

Jerry had turned Lucas down because the guy had no track record at that point to support taking over such an iconic property from a major corporation. Since then Jerry had optioned out the rights to Dino De Laurentiis. Dino got Jerry's approval because he promised he'd get Fellini to direct it.

I responded in disbelief, "You mean re-make *Flash Gordon* just like the comic strip? Not modernize it?" That's exactly what Dino wanted to do and what King Features agreed to, which I told Jerry was a flat-out horrible idea and a tragic waste of a great opportunity.

George Lucas found a brilliant way to salvage his vision. He realized if he didn't call it *Flash Gordon* he didn't need any rights to anything. He'd just change the name of the lead hero to something else, then essentially do exactly what he wanted to do in combining *Flash Gordon* Sci-fi with Kubrick's futuristic technology. Sure he'd lose the recognition factor of the iconic Buster Crabb character but at least he could fulfil his vision and who knows, maybe create a new iconic character of his own. George's first title was *The Adventures of Luke Starkiller*. Too 'hot' in the McLuhan sense and unlike Flash Gordon, the name Luke meant nothing to the audience so it didn't need to be in the title at all. The studio changed it to *The Star Wars*, which was later shortened to *Star Wars*. Cooler.

8. COUNTING HUGGIES

I finally married that "Italian girl" and moved into a new campsite, a suburban one-bedroom apartment in the town of Dobbs Ferry in Westchester County New York, just north of the city along the Hudson River. We soon had a beautiful little daughter. A daughter who needed a crib. And baby clothes. And formula. And a pediatrician. We converted the dining room to a nursery and with no room to eat in the tiny kitchen, we had to set up a folding bridge table in the living room.

If it sounds like we were poor it's because we were. With as little as we needed, I had no steady job to pay for any of it. Probably to keep from going insane I convinced myself that I did have a job, the job of cooking up movie ideas. What I would do with them and how I'd turn them into money to pay the bills I had no idea, but somehow it seemed better than the alternative which was to go out and get a nine to five job like "normal" people do in this situation.

Then the winter set in and to make things even more difficult the infamous oil embargo created a sudden, politically driven oil shortage that drove the prices of oil sky high. It didn't take long until we had no heat in our apartment. I learned from the frustrated building manager that the owners of our building, doctors, dentists, lawyers who were in it purely for the investment and tax advantages, had discovered that the New York state fine for not providing heat was far less than the jacked up oil bill for our apartment complex. If I had met any of these phantom owners I'd probably be finishing my parole after prison release right around now, but the immediate problem was keeping my family warm. We moved the baby's crib in front of the fireplace and I kept it going all night, with JoAnn and I crowded onto the couch under a pile of blankets. The next day I was clean out of firewood and after calling around realized I couldn't afford to buy the minimum half chord. So I did what I never thought I'd ever do. Steal. Like Jean Valjean in *Les Miserables*, I set out to find firewood piles behind nearby private houses and when I did, climbed their fences and tucked as many pieces under my coat as I could. Two more trips and we'd be good for another cold night. This went on for about another week when one of the tenants, who happened to be a lawyer, got the attention of the county executive and our heat was miraculously restored.

So it was back to work for me. Every night after dinner I'd sit back with my trusty yellow legal pad and Bic pen, then close my eyes and mentally free-form, searching through the old files stored deep in my brain for some inspiration for a movie. My files were already organized because pretty much everything in my memory had already been transformed into sci-fi movies somewhere in the storage process. Then I came across one that opened a doorway back to:

1957. Just as I'd about gotten over my radioactive movie-inspired fear of shrinking, my brother Gary came across an article about how to obtain fishing worms for free by jolting them out of our own backyard with electricity from our Lionel train transformer. So we waited until nightfall and snuck the transformer out into the yard and over to a large, round dirt area stamped into the lawn by our aboveground pool which had just been dismantled for the season. As per the instructions, we retrieved the garden hose and sprayed water over the area until all that dirt turned to mud. Gary then pounded a metal rod about a foot down into the center of the circle.

Then, like one of the mad scientists from our sci-fi movies, he plugged the train transformer into a socket at the base of the pool light, attached two wires to it, and fastened the other ends of the wires to the metal rod. The theory was that a jolt of electricity from the transformer would send juice through the rod and the soaked ground would act as a conductor to shock the worms. When they rose to the surface, we were to turn the pool light on so we could see them and gather them up into a coffee can. But we had to act fast because the light would repel them back into the ground.

I cautiously took my position on the far perimeter; Gary placed his thumb on the handle.

"You ready?"

I was too scared to talk so I just nodded from the darkness.

He gave it the juice. Not a sound. It seemed like nothing happened until he turned the flood light on illuminating hundreds of slimy, glistening worms, writhing out of the ground in a frenzy!

Gary shut the juice then quickly gathered worms into the can. Some of them were fried by the electricity, others had already started burrowing back into the mud.

"C'mon, help!"

I just stood there mesmerized. It was like I was watching a new sci-fi movie, only this one was in color and 3-D - and somehow I was right inside the action surrounded by thousands of worms! Then ten thousand! Then a million! And they all had giant mouths and teeth. And they screamed like pre-historic monsters while they squirmed in every direction, searching for flesh to devour!

CUT BACK TO: 1972

I frantically scrawled the word *Squirm* on my yellow pad. Then I stared at the word, then crossed it out. Still in my Pintoff-inspired McLuhan mode, I changed it to *SKWORM*.

As JoAnn ripped another wet Pamper off the baby, I set down the pad and called out to her.

"Hey Jo, whadda ya think of this? Millions of worms get jolted by a huge blast of electricity and become carnivorous monsters. S-K-W-O-R-M. SKWORM. Get it? Worms? Squirming worms?"

Her words resonated from the other room.

"That's the stupidest idea I ever heard in my life!"

Truth be told, JoAnn's reaction didn't faze me. But what did grab my attention was the fact that she was tearing off a recently changed 'Huggies' disposable diaper and pulling a fresh new one out of the box.

"What are you doing? You just changed her."

What she was doing was what any mother would do. Our little bundle had just wet another diaper, so, she was changing it. But it bothered me that these new disposable diapers went for 25 cents apiece which was a lot of money to just throw away in the trash basket. Check that, a lot of money to someone who had NO money coming in. No job. No income. A lot of money to someone who was also the supposed 'breadwinner' of this new family. The pressure was really getting to me.

"Can't you just let it steep a while?" I asked, instantly realizing what a stupid question that was, yet glad I asked it, because it brought my mental condition to the fore. Here I was with a wife and kid, bank account approaching zero, stealing firewood, counting twenty-five cent diapers and

Jeff Lieberman • Day Of The Living Me!

I'm dreaming up a movie about worms taking over a town? THAT is one fucked up mental condition. That one paragraph scribbled on a yellow legal pad was supposed to result in what, paying our rent? Our food bills? The electric bill? Gas and insurance for the car? AND for disposable diapers too?

I flipped the pad across the room and next morning I checked the want ads in the paper. Want ads? I didn't even know what category to look under. Anyone looking for someone who knows how to shoot a film and is also into 50s Sci-fi? I had to face it, I had no real marketable skill. I couldn't even type!

Then I remembered a man named Norman Turell who was the head of sales for King Features school distribution and was in charge of selling my film *The Ringer*. Norman not only loved my film but also saw something special in me and kept telling me I needed to meet his brother Saul, president of a film company I'd never heard of called Janus Films. I got hold of Norman and asked if he could set up that appointment with his brother. A half hour later Norman called back telling me to be at Janus at 11 AM the following day. I grabbed my Bic pen and jotted down the address, right under the word 'SKWORM.'

Next morning, I put on my only suit and took the train to Grand Central. From there I hoofed it up to 745 5th Ave, one of the most prestigious addresses in Manhattan at that time. It was located diagonally across from The Plaza Hotel and next door to the General Motors building and the Sherry Netherland hotel.

Since Norman never said anything about a job opening, my hope was that his brother Saul could give me some guidance, maybe even make some phone calls on my behalf. That alone would be worth putting on a suit for.

I introduced myself at the front desk and was told that Mr. Turell was out of the office and running late and I should just take a seat. I waited until 11:30 and still no sign of him. Fuck this I figured, you'd think the guy would've at least had the decency to cancel. When I got up to leave, Saul came blasting through the door like a hurricane, hair disheveled, suitcase in one hand, stuffed file folder in the other. He freed up a finger to shake hands with, then spoke in a rapid fire, clipped fashion that was hard to understand. From what I gathered, he was apologizing about keeping me waiting, and explaining that his brother Norman told him all about me and surprisingly, that he'd seen my film 'The Ringer' and was very impressed with it. Then he stopped abruptly and asked, "Hungry?"

I checked my watch as if I had another appointment later on other than taking the train home, then shrugged and said, "Sure."

Adventures of a Subversive Cult Filmmaker from the Golden Age.

And just like that my half hour courtesy meeting morphed into a lunch at the upscale NYU Club, which lasted so long that by the time Saul called for the check, the waiters were already setting the tables for dinner. Saul's mind ran at a thousand miles per hour and you really had to concentrate to get the gist of what he was saying because he would skip over the dots that would make him easier to follow.

But I was able to quickly adapt to his edit speak, realizing this guy was very very smart and the onus was on me to keep up with him. For his part, he seemed riveted by my every word, like I was some sage of the times, like I was onto something that he wanted in on. He actually said it. Not quite that way but he said he wanted to 'ride on my back.'

Ride on my back? I thought. He was president of this big company and I was just some young broke desperate schmuck pounding the pavement looking for work. He extrapolated otherwise from The Ringer?

He said he wanted to hire me and even though there were no particular positions to fill, he did have something in mind which he'd tell me about on Monday when he wanted me to start. Then he asked how much I needed. I told him I didn't need a paycheck, just pay my bills and take that enormous pressure off me. He said to tally up my expenses and then he'd give them to his accountant who'll calculate how much I had to make in gross income in order to have enough money left over after taxes to cover my nut. With that, he slapped his hand on the table and said, "See ya Monday?" And that was it.

As I headed down Fifth Avenue to make the train, I wasn't sure exactly what just happened, but I did feel that albatross pulling away from my neck and flying off to find some other poor soul to land on.

When I arrived home from the station I did my best Fred McMurray-Ozzie Nelson-Danny Thomas entrance as I faked tossing an imaginary hat onto our antique coatrack.

"Honey I'm home!"

"Did you get the job?"

"What job? There was no job."

"Can he at least help you?"

"He did. He hired me."

"You said…"

"There was no job. And there isn't. So he made one up for me."

"Doing what?"

"No clue. I'll find out Monday when I start."

She threw her arms around me. "You're such a jerk."

We just stood there hugging. The pressure was off me. Her too. No more counting pampers. But little did I realize...

9. I WAS ABOUT TO ENTER
...THE TWILIGHT ZONE!

That Monday at Janus Films, Saul started me off with a rundown of what the company was all about. He and his partner William Becker built the label into a prestigious film distribution company known for releasing 'art films,' mostly foreign, through specialty art house theaters, colleges and arts-oriented television networks like PBS. Their bread and butter was renting out 16mm prints of classic movies from the collection; the early Bergman films *Seventh Seal* and *The Magician*, The Early Hitchcocks like *The Thirty Nine Steps*, Fellini's *La Strada*, Truffaut's *Jules and Jim* and *Two English Girls*, and so on. Though it was very profitable, they'd reached a plateau and there was very little growth potential from that point on. All the titles that could be sold to American television to play in their entirety had already been exploited. So the only way to expand was to acquire new properties, which was getting very competitive because many other companies were forming to get in on the same non-theatrical market and syndicated TV.

That's where I came in. Saul wanted me to figure out ways to create new product from what Janus already owned. Re-package them into series, cut them up into half hours, anything I could think of that would result in the creation of new titles, which Janus could then copyright and sell. Saul referred to the process as "mining for gold." He could've called it recycling, or re-purposing but those terms weren't popularized yet.

After screening a few of the feature movies Janus acquired from the Rank Organization, one of them stood out to me. It was a 1955 movie called *A Kid for Two Farthings*, written by Wolf Mankowitz from his own novel and directed by Carol Reed. The story is set in one of mid-century London's lower class areas filled with small shops and street vendors. A young boy, Joe, hears a tale from an old Jewish tailor named Mr. Kandinsky about these mythical creatures called unicorns and how they actually exist and can grant any wish. Joe spots a goat in the market that seems to have a horn jutting out from the middle of his head, believes it's a unicorn, and buys it, for two farthings.

The movie itself was God-awful with a story line about a wrestler in love with a sexy blonde played by Diana Dors. But I realized if I could cut all that stuff out and only focus on the sub plot of old Kandinsky and his little friend Joe who uses the unicorn to make a wish for the old man to get a steam iron that he believes will change his life, it'd make for a nice little children's film. So I took one of our 16mm prints and cut it down myself on the movieola that was set up in back of the conference room. To make the narrative work in this new form I wrote voice over dialogue to bridge the disconnected scenes, then brought in New York syndicated talk radio personality Barry Gray to narrate. The result was good enough to sell to the CBS network for their Saturday afternoon children's theater, which more than paid for my salary for the next two years. Saul was now officially comfortable that the bet he made on me was already paying off.

One day Saul introduced me to a young man about my age name Leonard Maltin. Even at such an early stage in his career, Leonard had shown an almost encyclopedic knowledge of all things movies. He could name the title, the year made, the stars, writers and directors of pretty much every movie that was ever made. At least it seemed that way. Saul saw him as a great research tool, a shortcut to getting quick answers on issues like rights holders, negative access, everything so Saul put Leonard on retainer so we could call him any time and ask him a question. On the rare occasions Maltin couldn't answer on the spot, he'd check in with his own network of film geeks and usually have an answer within a few hours. We used him in the same way we use the Internet today, so in a sense he was our human Google, decades before search engines existed. It's no wonder he went on to be one of the top film critics of the modern era.

Now that Saul was confident in my gold mining skills, he had another area he wanted me to explore. He explained that since colleges were already renting Janus's movies on a regular basis, we had a big list of potential customers if we could create something new out of those classics.

"Okay then," I said, "How 'bout giving the film professors some kind of a teaching aide to supplement their courses on those movies and on movies in general? Using clips from all the classics to explain how stuff is done? And the films we use will be mainly ours." He was all ears so I continued.

"Break it up into separate basic subjects, like writing, directing, camera work, editing. And show examples of each using clips from the masters."

Saul slapped his open hand on the table, which was his signal to go ahead full steam.

This was the birth of *The Art of Film*, a multi-part series of twenty-minute shows using clips from the Janus collection to illustrate artistic techniques used by the great filmmakers. We decided to start with six twenty-minute segments, each focused on a different topic. Volume one was "The Camera." Volume Two, "The Edited Image." Then "The Actor," "Music and Sound," "The Writer," and "The Director."

Since it would all be comprised of clips, it called for a voiceover narrator and to me there was only one voice for it. The voice that kept me glued to the television for a half hour every week when I was younger. The voice that carried more authority than any teacher I'd ever had. A man who could make us believe pretty much anything, even that there could really be a place called *The Twilight Zone*.

It just so happened that a close friend of mine named Fred Berner had Rod Serling as a media professor when he attended Ithaca College. Rod was living on Lake Cayuga New York, not far from the college. Out of courtesy Rod accepted a call from me.

He was very formal at first, bombarding me with questions about the project and how it would be used since if he agreed he'd be doing this for very short money at the time. He ranked number one in credibility in advertising surveys, and his "Mazda Performs" commericals were fetching six figures for a thirty second spot. And that's in early 1970's money.

After another long phone call, Rod felt sufficiently comfortable with both the project and me and his personality brightened. Then out of nowhere he said,

"Two Polacks and a Chinaman walk into a bar ..."

I instantly cracked up. Not because it was politically incorrect since that whole concept only emerged two decades later, but I mean, this was Rod Serling telling me a Polish joke! Same distinctive voice and delivery cadence as he did throughout my formative years watching *The Twilight Zone*! Rod thought I was laughing at the joke itself, not the fact that it was Rod Serling telling it. And the more I laughed, the more Polish jokes he told me. So, we kind of bonded over the love of Polish jokes. Or so he thought. He agreed to narrate the first two pilot episodes with the provision we do it at Ithaca college and use some of the students in the film department to help out. We arranged to meet in front of the communications building at a set time. Before I hung up, I dead panned, "Hold it, how will I recognize you?"

The obvious joke was that his was one of the most familiar faces in showbiz at the time. Rod didn't miss a beat.

"Excellent point. Tell you what Jeff, I'll be wearing a red carnation in my left lapel."

So I got on a plane and flew up to Ithaca, then took a car to the college, arriving at the agreed upon spot as planned. And there he was, much shorter than I had imagined him, and damn if he wasn't wearing a red carnation in his left lapel!

I approached him, all the while keeping up the ruse that I'm searching around for this Rod Serling guy who said he'd be wearing a red carnation in his left lapel so I could identify him from the crowd.

As I got close to him, without making eye contact, I pretended to notice the red flower and leaned in to study it.

"Is that a carnation?"

"Yes it is."

"Then you must be Rod Serling!"

Rod cracked a big smile and we did that shake-hands-and-then-shake-each others-shoulders thing that guys did to show manly affection, long before it was replaced by the full-on hug.

Rod was a totally different person than the personality he presented to the public. At least to me he was. Not a minute went by when one of us wasn't hitting the other with a joke, or doing stupid schtick drawn from sources like The Three Stooges, or the Marx brothers. I'd open a door for Rod and say, "After you." Then he'd say, "No, after you." Then I'd say, "No, I insist!" At which point he'd proceed only to be cut off by me rushing in in front of him, Three Stooges style.

The recording sessions went great and I headed back to the city with the tapes. The two pilot episodes sold immediately to a distributor who specialized in educational films for high schools and colleges. This meant that we were green lit for four more twenty-minute episodes.

Rod tried to couple his visits to New York City with other business and we put him up at his favorite place, the St. Regis in mid-town. One night at the famous King Cole bar, I took a sip of my drink and then asked a question that had been bothering me for some time.

Adventures of a Subversive Cult Filmmaker from the Golden Age.

"So Rod, one of the films we'll be covering is '*The Dead of Night*, British anthology film from the 40's."

He nodded, "Forty-five I'd guess. Know it well."

"So one of the stories we're covering is about a ventriloquist who's dummy becomes his alter ego. Didn't you do a Twilight Zone episode on that same concept?"

"Yep. The Dummy."

"So you ripped that off from *The Dead of Night*?"

Rod picked up his drink and with a big grin said, "When you steal, steal from the best."

Then he toasted my glass.

Ironically, more people have stolen from Rod Serling over the years than any other writer I can think of.

Saul and I wrote the copy for all six episodes together, with Saul concentrating on the overall movie the scenes were taken from for context while I focused on the specific cinema techniques employed. We chose the subject 'The Edited Image' as the next title to tackle for *The Art of Film* series and included footage from Leni Riefenstahl's *Olympiad*. As much as I hated Riefenstahl for being Hitler's personal Nazi propaganda filmmaker, I appreciated her contribution to the edited image and her important place in film history. Her pioneering work in *Olympiad*, the German propaganda documentary of the 1939 Olympics, displayed the first use of the montage to extend or contract time in sports and was used expertly in the diving sequences. These same techniques are still used today in sports broadcasts throughout the world.

Late one morning I was working in the editing room when the phone rang. It was Saul informing me that Leni Riefenstahl was in his office! He explained she was on her way to Los Angeles and made a special stopover in New York just to see what I've done with her film.

My pulse went into overdrive. I told Saul that if I came into his office and he introduced me to her and she reached out her hand, there's a fifty-fifty chance of me either shaking it, or grabbing it tight as I could and whipping her out his fifth floor window onto Fifth Avenue. I was dead serious and he knew it.

Saul stammered, trying not to let on what I was saying on the phone, then faked it with Ms. Fraulein that I had a lunch appointment (it was 11:30 AM) and was just running out the door.

CUT TO: Magno Sound, the mid-town Manhattan recording studio where Rod was cranking out his narration for "The Art of Film episode three: The Edited Image."

A chain smoker to a fault, Rod literally used the embers of his last cigarette to light up the next one in what must have been at least a four pack a day habit. And it took a real toll on his voice, giving him that deep raspy sound that lent itself so well to narration while playing havoc with his lungs and heart. After a particularly violent coughing fit he looked up at me and said, "These things are gonna kill me.'

"Why don't you quit?"

"I can't."

And he said it with such certainty it also meant it was the end of the conversation and he was resigned to his fate.

Before each take he'd have to clear his throat and cough a few times before he spoke. A lit cigarette was always close at hand, which he immediately reached for after each paragraph of copy was laid down.

But when he turned the script page to the next film and read the copy, Olympiad and introduced the filmmaker as "Leni Riefenstahl, out of nowhere he added "That Nazi cunt!" His face flushed with rage as he got up from his chair and slammed down his script. "Do you know who the fuck she is? I won't read this! I'm not doing this."

Perfect time to call a coffee break. I led Rod out to a hallway where it was just the two of us, face-to-face and man-to-man.

I told him that the purpose of this project was to expose young audiences to the art of film. Riefenstahl's art had to be separated from her as a person. Then I recounted the story of the frauline's visit to the Janus offices.

When I finished, Rod looked at me and nodded slightly, then crushed out his cigarette in one of those sandy, hallway ashtrays. "Too bad you didn't throw her out that window."

As we re-entered the studio I made sure to alert everyone there'd better not be any screw-ups because I had a gut feeling Rod only intended to do this once. And if you ever get a chance to see 'The Art of Film' and that one episode, you'll notice how his reading for 'Olympiad' was distinctly different than all the rest as he struggled to spit out the name of "that Nazi cunt!"

Unfortunately Rod was right about his cigarette habit and two years later it finally killed him at age 50. Too soon my friend.

Adventures of a Subversive Cult Filmmaker from the Golden Age.

The Unicorn created from the feature movie *A Kid for two Farthings*

Me directing Rod Serling narration for *The Art of Film*

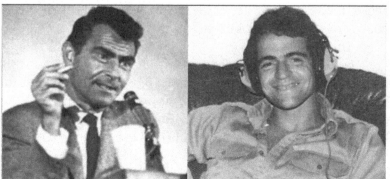

10. JOHN LENNON, KING KONG AND THE WORLD TRADE CENTER

Saul informed me that Janus acquired the rights to *King Kong*, the 1939 black and white RKO classic. He asked me to see if there was any way to exploit it besides the TV syndication his sales guy was in the process of making. I loved that movie and must have seen it more than ten times on *The Million Dollar Movie*, but I decided to screen it again with an eye toward mining gold.

I dug out a joint I kept in my desk drawer, then headed to the elevators for a little toke in Central park before I dove into *King Kong*.

Janus Films now shared space with Lee Radziwill's architectural and design firm. At least once a week Lee's sister, Jackie Kennedy Onassis, came up to fetch Lee for lunch, and this time I found myself entering the elevator with them.

They were two standard issue, uptight, never talk in elevators types so when the doors slid closed, they both clammed up and looked straight ahead. It was just the three of us, me and the Bouviers. We all realized nobody had pressed the button, so I broke the silence.

"Lobby?"

Jackie allowed me a slight nod while she kept her focus on her reflection on the shiny closed door. As I pressed the button, I suddenly started channeling Mel Blank's Daffy Duck as an elevator operator, emphasizing that exaggerated lisp. "Going down, shoes, socks, mops and lingerie!" They both cracked up, but like those super uptight people who internalize their sneezes, they instantly defaulted back to their straight-ahead zombie stares.

Adventures of a Subversive Cult Filmmaker from the Golden Age.

I walked through the lobby and out the revolving doors to the street with them and they smiled as we parted ways with them continuing down Fifth Avenue while I jaywalked across Fifth to the Plaza Hotel fountain outside Central Park.

On sunny days like that one there were always lots of street performers entertaining the tourists. I always looked out for this one lively little French guy in white mime make-up who'd wow the crowds with stunts like stretching a tight rope between two trees then walking over their heads. He would also juggle and ride around the fountain on a unicycle, then pass his hat for donations. I got to know him by his first name, which was Philippe, which I shortened to 'Phil.' Sometimes I'd serve as a shill for him.

"Hey Phil, bet ya can't go backwards to the other tree!"

As I passed the Plaza fountain on my way to the park, Phil scooted by on his unicycle in white mime face. He made for a very Felliniesque image as he waved and smiled knowingly, like he knew where I was headed. And why.

I passed a lonely looking Ed Sullivan on a park bench feeding the pigeons, alone in his thoughts. Once in the park I continued past the zoo, past my old phone booth- A.K.A. the Jeff Lieberman and Associates main office - to a secluded spot I remembered at the back of the building. I checked to make sure the coast was clear, lit up the joint, took a few tokes, then backtracked to the Janus screening room where I slipped on my imaginary gold mining helmet and signaled for the projectionist to roll the first reel of *King Kong*.

First thing that came to me was realizing that the viewer needed to see the whole movie for it to have any impact, so cutting it up, or making an abridged version, say, for children's television was out of the question. But there was a simple overriding theme in the movie that had never been apparent to me watching it in my youth. The movie wasn't really about a monster gorilla; it was about the white man's basic fear of the black man. Think about it, a giant black beast in human form taken from the wilds of Africa in chains. On top of that, the fear of interracial romance was illustrated by the strange relationship between the beast and the blonde, lily-white Faye Wray. So I focused on looking for the best medium to present that human story.

The answer was Broadway. A Broadway musical!

In a flash I envisioned it all, klieg lights on opening night with the words *King Kong* scrawled across the theater marquee. I pictured two William

Jeff Lieberman • Day Of The Living Me!

Morris agents planning a guy adventure to Club Med, then one suggesting something different. Something daring. A real African safari. Of course, it'd be on their safari that they discover *King Kong* which they proclaim will be the biggest client the agency ever had.

In place of the natives in the movie playing drums and dancing and chanting to summon the God Kong, I pictured a long chorus line of black Motown singers, all wearing identical pink satin tuxedos, dancing in unison like the Temptations. Of course, this being Broadway, you could never actually *see* the giant gorilla back at that time, but you'd always feel his presence through the use of shadows, sound effects and actors looking up at him just off stage.

Okay, so what did I know about Broadway? As much as Charlie Baxter knew about catering food to a half-million people at Woodstock. Nada. Gornisht. Zip. But luck would have it that William Becker, the chairman of Janus, was married to Patricia Birch, the choreographer of *Grease*, among many other Broadway musical hits. So getting a show mounted around *King Kong* was not that far-fetched an idea. I knew enough, however, not to bring it up to Becker or Saul until it was something more than just a pipe dream.

My father, Irving Lieberman, was a fundraiser for various charitable organizations and during this period he was working for the American Parkinson's Disease Association. Dad had a knack for attracting the biggest names in both industry and show business to serve as 'guests of honor' at his fundraising dinners, which were usually held at the Waldorf Astoria hotel. He knew that it was not the disease or cause that inspired important and wealthy people to pony up thousands of dollars for a table at these events. They did it to pay homage to (score points with) the guest of honor. In my father's words, "They don't care if the cause is cancer or prickly heat; it's the guest of honor and the people who feel they owe him, or want something from him, that counts."

Fate would have it that my father got Ahmet Ertegun to commit to the guest of honor title at one of his Waldorf galas. My reaction to his name was, Ahmet who? I'd never heard of him. But of course I'd heard of Atlantic records who took over releasing the Rolling Stones along with a dozen other major name acts, so when my father told me Ahmet was the founder of the company, I thought that was pretty cool.

I hated putting on a tie let alone a monkey suit, but JoAnn and I attended these black tie affairs mainly because we'd get a free high-class dinner along with top shelf entertainment, all for the cost of a baby sitter.

Adventures of a Subversive Cult Filmmaker from the Golden Age.

Sometimes we'd even get a fancy room in the Waldorf towers thrown in. I didn't actually own a tuxedo so I made do with the only suit I did own - an off-the-rack Barney's dark brown, tweed number sporting the ultra wide lapels of the times along with a fashionable bib wide tie.

As usual for these occasions I toked up in the restroom so I could make it through the endless speeches sandwiched between dessert and the entertainment. But as soon as we entered the grand ballroom it was clear this particular fundraiser was different than any of the others my dad produced. Everyone who was ANYONE in the music business was either there ("Look, there's Bette Midler!", "check it out, Paul Simon, he's so short!") or were sending closed-circuit apologies explaining why they couldn't make it. Evidently Ahmet was not only president of Atlantic records, but was loved and respected by pretty much everyone in the business.

As was his ritual at these things, my father summoned JoAnn and I to the cordoned off V.I.P. area to introduce us to the guest of honor. Last time he did this was to meet his previous guest of honor, William Randolph Hearst Jr., who turned out to be a pretty cool guy and wound up being a close friend of my dad's.

There was a short line of people waiting to pay respects to Ahmet and among them was a longhaired fellow in white sneakers sporting a gold sheriff's badge pinned to his black jacket lapel. Then I realized it was none other than John Lennon.

I glanced in his eyes and when he caught a glimpse of mine there was an instant recognition that we were both wasted. Potheads always know when they encounter a fellow stoner. He grinned and nodded and I did the same, then he extended his hand and said, "John." And I said, "Jeff" and we shook.

After my dad introduced JoAnn and I to Ahmet, we stepped away to let John take his turn. As we headed back into the ballroom to find our table I said to JoAnn.

"Why didn't he have to wear a suit and tie like I do?"

"Because he's John Lennon."

"Who made the rule that if you're a big celebrity the term 'black tie' doesn't apply to you and you can wear whatever you want while everyone else has to wear a monkey suit?"

Monkey suit. The words triggered something. Gorilla suit. Gorillas. *King Kong*! *King Kong* on Broadway. Music and lyrics by John Lennon!

"Be right back," I said to JoAnn. I'll meet you at our table."

Jeff Lieberman • Day Of The Living Me!

Without a moment's thought about the impropriety of what I was about to do, JoAnn watched dumbfounded as I turned back to the VIP area.

I located John who was now surrounded by a horde of kiss-ass record executives eager to shake his hand. I called out, "John!"

He turned around and recognized me from a minute ago and smiled like we were old friends. He was looking for an excuse to get away from all those suits and I inadvertently gave him one. I took him aside for a private chat.

"You know the movie *King Kong*, right?"

"I do."

"Do you know what it was really about?"

"Well certainly. The white man's fear of the black man."

"Bingo!"

That launched me into a rap about how "my" company Janus (which he'd heard of, thank God) owned the rights to *King Kong*, and that I wanted to do a Broadway show based on the movie. Then I babbled on about the Klieg lights, the pink tuxedoed Motown chorus line, the two William Morris agents and Pat Birch the choreographer. John held this Mona Lisa like tight smile, which made it hard for me to tell if he was really listening, or just being polite.

By now, the legions of record execs were wondering who was this kid getting so much face time with John Lennon? Then another idea hit me.

"To drive the racial message home, how 'bout getting Stevie Wonder to do the black music and you do the white music!"

I finally got some feedback. "So me and Stevie would work together on the score."

"Yeah, but you both write separate stuff, separate parts. Like Stevie's sort of the musical voice of *King Kong*, and you're the white western civilization that captures him."

Before John could respond, everyone was summoned to take their seats at the tables. And sure enough, JoAnn and I were seated at the same freaking table as John and Yoko! At least I thought it was Yoko but it turned out to be an Asian lady named Mai Pang, John's girlfriend during his so called "lost weekend" two year split with Yoko. The photographer took a picture of all of us, then JoAnn and I took our seats.

During dinner John showed no sign of wanting to continue the conversation and by the time dessert arrived my elation was being replaced by regret. I started to think John's half smile was probably just him trying to politely endure my stupid idea while taking refuge from the record executives. Or worse, he was goofing on me, watching this kid make a total jerk out of himself. Or both. Would it get back to my father that his son was bothering John Lennon at the Ahmet Ertegun dinner? Maybe it already had. I couldn't wait to get out of there.

Too embarrassed to tell JoAnn the truth, I made up some lame excuse to leave early. "Let's beat the coat check lines. Gonna be a nightmare."

By the time we got home I was so overcome with paranoia I couldn't get to sleep. I paced the apartment beating myself up about what a schmuck I was to do that and for the first time actually reconsidered my pot use. Finally around 2:30 A.M. the phone rang.

I just stared at the receiver and let it ring again because in my family it could only mean one thing, someone just died. When the ringing finally woke JoAnn she sat up and looked at me.

"Aren't you gonna answer it?"

"Probably wrong number."

"Well pick it up and see!"

I lifted the receiver and mustered a weak, "Hello?"

"What did you say to John Lennon last night?" asked the gruff male voice on the other end. John Lennon. Okay, nobody died, but this was bad. Really bad. My fears had been confirmed. I tried to play dumb.

"Who's calling?" He said he was an executive from RCA records. Then came the bomb.

"Whatever it is you said, John wants to meet for lunch tomorrow, twelve noon at Danny's Hideaway. He's bringing his lawyer. Something about *King Kong*?"

I played it cool.

"Oh, okay. Sure. Twelve noon? Got it. I'll also bring Saul Turell, he's the president of Janus."

I hung up the phone, shell shocked.

"Who was it?"

"Holy. Shit."

"What happened?"

"Holy shit!"

I explained it all to her, then went back to pacing the apartment while she went back to sleep. I made myself some coffee, just chomping at the bit to get to the office to tell Saul the news.

I took an early train and arrived at Janus before Saul, but Bill Becker was there so I broke it all to him. Bill grinned from ear to ear at the news. He had a lot of experience with Broadway and thought just music by John

Lennon, with or without Stevie Wonder, would guarantee financing of such a well-known property as *King Kong*. He got right on the phone and called his wife Patricia Birch, who confirmed Bill's analysis, then Pat in turn called Hal Prince who immediately threw his director's hat into the ring. So that was it, Tony award winning director, the choreographer of *Grease*, and John freaking Lennon. Putting together a Broadway show was easy! I could already see those Klieg lights on opening night. And this time I'd spring for a tux!

Saul finally arrived and I followed him into his office and excitedly repeated what I told Bill. But he didn't react the way Bill did. In fact, he didn't say a word. What the fuck? Wasn't this exactly what he hired me for, to mine gold? And didn't I just hit the mother lode?

"It's not our gold to mine yet," he said, before closing the door for privacy.

"What? You said we had the rights!"

He said that we do. But only to 16 millimeter distribution and TV. But he assured me nobody else has any other rights and he can go to the head lawyer of General Tires, which owned RKO and their entire library including *King Kong* and *Citizen Kane* and get the clearance we needed.

I asked myself why Saul hadn't told me this beforehand but the way he was handling this made the answer fairly obvious. He didn't want to dampen my enthusiasm with legalities. His M.O. with me was to tell me just enough to get me in creative gear, and then if I came up with something interesting, he'd step in and do his best to make it happen. Had he told me we didn't actually have the rights to adapt *King Kong* to a Broadway show, there's no way I would've pitched John Lennon on it.

"Saul, I'm supposed to be meeting John at Danny's Hideaway at noon!"

Saul's eyes widened. He grabbed his phone and called the RKO lawyer and made it imperative that he meet us for an 'early lunch' (11:00 am) at the Sherry Netherland, which was one short block up fifth avenue from our office.

In those days the Sherry-Netherland Hotel was very formal and you couldn't even step into the ground floor restaurant without a coat and tie. I had neither, so the maître de dug into the lost and found pile and the best he could do was a Nehru-collared, 46-long, powder blue jacket speckled with a smattering of vintage gravy stains.

I had no other choice but to put it on, and then roll up the sleeves, achieving the 'Dopey' from the Seven Dwarves look. Saul and I proceeded into the restaurant and joined the only seated patron, a rotund, cherubic, white-haired, old school Irish gentleman sporting very lawyerly suspenders.

Adventures of a Subversive Cult Filmmaker from the Golden Age.

The waiter brought us menus but I wasn't really interested in eating. My mission was to get this guy to verbally sign off on what we needed, then grab a cab to Danny's Hideaway on 45th street. When I finished my presentation he seemed very impressed, especially with the John Lennon attachment. But then he took a sip of water, set his glass down and uttered the one word I didn't want to hear.

"However…"

That was the loudest "HOWEVER" I ever heard!

"… there's another party interested in remaking the movie."

Remaking the movie?! That's the dumbest idea I ever heard! What was wrong with the last movie, that it's not in color? I figured it should be easy to talk this guy out of making that deal. He told us the person who wanted to remake the movie hadn't actually put up any money yet and in fact his option deadline was nearing. Well then, this should've been a no-brainer because we were for real and had the money to back it up!

But then he went back to that dreaded word: "However, if he were to come through, his agreement calls for an exclusive on *King Kong* which would preclude any Broadway interpretation."

Saul asked for the amount of the advance this phantom person was supposed to put up and the Lawyer said it was twenty-five thousand dollars, which in 1974 was a boatload of money to plop down on something that may or may not come to fruition. Gotta hand it to Saul. He offered to go back up to the Janus offices and cut a check for 25K right then and there on a handshake.

The lawyer was tempted to take the bird in the hand offer, but he said the interested party is someone who must be taken seriously and he's just going to have to wait. I looked at my watch, I had fifteen more minutes.

"Can you at least tell us who it is?"

"Dino De Laurentiis."

My blood ran cold. Dino again! First *Flash Gordon* and now this! I never even met the man and it seemed like he was out to sabotage me. But the hard reality was, if Dino De Laurentiis wants to remake *King Kong*, he's gonna remake *King Kong*, no ifs ands or buts. Now I not only looked like Dopey, I also felt like Dopey because I had to walk back up to the office and cancel the meeting with John Lennon.

And tell his lawyer what? We didn't have the rights to *King Kong* after all?

That night, JoAnn did everything she could to get me out of my funk.

Jeff Lieberman • Day Of The Living Me!

I was so close to changing the course of history. At least Broadway history. Okay, at least my own history anyway.

In an attempt to get my mind off it all, JoAnn flipped on the news. The big story of the night was that someone actually walked between the two new World Trade Center towers on a tightrope. They showed a clip of it, then interviewed the daredevil who pulled this off. It was Phil, the French mime from the Plaza fountain, or 'Philippe Petit' as the newscaster revealed.

"Holy crap, I know that guy!"

To which JoAnn said, "That figures."

JoAnn, me, John Lennon and my tie.

Philippe Petit at Plaza Fountain

11. "A COUPLE OF DICKS"

It was autumn of 1974 and the financial security Janus afforded me enabled me to get back to my obsession with dreaming up crazy movie ideas.

My fellow School of Visual Arts alum Marc Rubin and I had maintained our friendship since the Gatoraide commercial and were hell bent on writing the next great American movie comedy. Both big fans of Kubrick's *Dr. Strangelove*, we naturally gravitated to black comedy in the form of political and social satire. Marc was freelance writing for the National Lampoon while still maintaining his day job in advertising so we'd kick around ideas at night, mostly over the phone.

The women's liberation movement was gaining traction on a national level and the opposing attitudes and rising militancy over gender roles and identity seemed the perfect arena for our particular brand of humor.

Our pencil sketch story arch was to have a very macho, twenty-something cliché "male chauvinist pig" as the term was being coined at the time, learn first hand what it's like to be a woman and on the receiving end of the same misogynist behavior he's been dishing out to the opposite sex since puberty. This was eight years before *Tootsie* would tackle the same subject. The best way to show a man what it's like to be a woman is to make him walk a mile in her shoes. Literally. But unlike Dustin Hoffman's *Tootsie* character Michael Dorsey, who willingly dressed in drag to land an acting role, our main character, Tony Macherella, would never dress like a woman in a million years. Well, unless it was Halloween. So, we needed a device to get Tony into a dress.

"What if he got a sex change?"

Jeff Lieberman • Day Of The Living Me!

"No way he'd to that."

"Okay, then by accident."

We both laughed out loud. The outrageousness of the concept of someone getting a sex change by mistake immediately informed us of how over-the-top our satire would have to be in order for it to work. But it also provided us with the added bonus that it had the potential to offend pretty much everyone: feminists, gays, straight macho homophobes, even the transgender community, you name it. And it possessed the same irreverent take-no-prisoners brand of satire that distinguished the *Lampoon* at the time.

We gifted our Tony character with a hernia, which he suffered while cheating on his girlfriend and trying out a contorted sex position he read about in the *Kama Sutra*. Tony wound up in the emergency room of a grossly understaffed and overcrowded city hospital where major surgical screw-ups like scalpels left in stomachs or removals of wrong kidneys were commonplace. Then, as fate would have it, in a comedy of errors involving two incompetent orderlies and switched gurneys, instead of a hernia operation, Tony got a full sex change, the ultimate nightmare for a *gavone* from the Bronx. Our working title was *Pink and Blue*.

When we finished our story treatment we looked for feedback from colleagues. One of them, a friend of mine from childhood who was working as a sports writer, excitedly alerted me that he'd slipped our thirty pages to a hot young New York actor named Robert DeNiro who was very intrigued by the role of Tony Macherella. I was already familiar with DeNiro's work from the movie *Mean Streets* and knew from the press that this still relatively unknown actor had been cast to play the young Vito Corleone in *The Godfather: Part II*, which would be premiering in just a few months. I arranged to meet Robert at the Riviera Café in the Sheridan Square area of Greenwich Village.

We seemed to hit it off well right away, with Robert preferring I call him "Bob." It was clear to me he'd been putting a lot of thought into our treatment when he asked some very pertinent questions about the character of Tony.

Soon our conversation focused on a key transitional scene in our story which took place at a real-life, notorious, New York City drag club called Club 82. Five minutes later we were hailing a cab to 82 Fourth Street to do some on-the-ground research.

In our tragicomedy, the sexually transformed Tony is told by his personal transition counselor that the accidental procedure he endured, although most unfortunate, cannot be reversed, and that the estrogen

Adventures of a Subversive Cult Filmmaker from the Golden Age.

hormone therapy he's been receiving meant his breasts would continue to fill out, his facial hair would disappear and he'd be a woman, at least anatomically, from then on. The counselor recommends that for Tony's mental wellbeing he needed to transition his gender identity as well. He would need to stop behaving like the macho Tony, stop covering up the fact that he had breasts, stop wearing men's clothing altogether and "come out' as a woman named "Toni." The therapist suggested the best place to present Toni's new self was a downtown drag night spot called Club 82, where she could wear a dress and make-up and even high heels, and sort of ease her way into her new gender identity without fear of ridicule or judgment from other patrons. Sort of a halfway house step towards her full transition to womanhood.

Like virtually every nightclub in New York City with a cabaret license in the 1970's, The 82 was not so secretly owned by my Little Italy friend, Genovese crime family under boss Matthew 'Matty the Horse' Ianniello.

The club was managed by two women named Tommy and Butch, both old, tough-looking "Bull Dykes" as they were referred to in those pre-politically correct days, along with an all dyke staff of construction worker and biker types, all sporting tattoos and pumped-up muscles.

Pre-Blondie Deborah Harry, Lou Reed and David Bowie were frequent patrons taking this walk on the wild side, and were occasional performers as well, as were The New York Dolls featuring lead singer David Johansen in full drag. In fact, the Doll's raucous first performance on the 82 stage just might have officially ushered in the "glam rock" phase of 1970's to 1980's.

When Bob and I descended the stairs to the cavernous, smoke-filled 82, the place was packed and electrified by the new chart-busting Soul Searchers disco anthem "Get out your whistle and blow" blaring from banks of speakers. We waded through a sea of multi-colored, bouffant-teased and heavily sprayed hair-do's bobbing up and down. If you've ever been to a hospital morgue, you'd know how hard it is to adjust to the fact that all the people lying around you under white sheets on those gurneys are no longer patients, they're actually dead. In this case it was just as hard to adjust to the fact that virtually every one of these women on the dance floor were actually men.

Bob and I finally made it to the bar, found two empty stools side by side and instantly drew odd looks from the patrons around us because everything about us screamed "straight!"

Our first piece of business was to order drinks. We waved to our very butch bartender whom we learned from a nearby patron also calling out for drinks was named Erwin. But Erwin looked right past us like we were invisible. We couldn't believe it, she was outright ignoring us. Why? Clearly because we were men. Straight men. My first experience with blatant sexual discrimination. Too bad I didn't save that telephone number JoAnn made me tear up. One call to Joe and Matty and it would've been drinks on the house all night.

We both started slapping our palms on the bar for some attention.

"Ay Erwin! Can we get a drink over here? Hello!"

Erwin finally came over and reluctantly took our orders. Then we swiveled in our stools to take in the scene before us. Neither of us had ever seen anything like this. A band of men on stage in full drag, transvestites, transsexuals, gay men and sailors, lots of sailors on leave from the west side docks looking to score, all gyrating to the music. We knocked back our first drinks pretty quickly and pounded our glasses down hard, cowboy movie style to make it clear to Erwin we needed refills.

Just then a six foot two drag queen pulled up along side me and ordered a Shirley Temple. She got waited on immediately. She was built like a linebacker and might very well have played some college ball earlier on. I couldn't help stare at the thickly layered makeup pasted over her bumpy five o'clock shadow, her size 13 high heels, sequined mini skirt and mile high teased up hair-do. But when she sensed me staring, I quickly shifted my gaze to the mirror behind the bar, then elbowed Bob so he could see what I was seeing.

Our reflections amounted to what's known in movie lingo as a three shot; the drag queen and Bob, and me sandwiched between them. Bob looked down at his drink and whispered to me from the side of his mouth. "So Tony's Uncle Enzo comes here alone. Maybe all the time but that's another story. He comes up to this bar and recognizes his nephew Tony, that guy next to you."

Uncle Enzo? There was no Uncle Enzo in our treatment. Bob was inventing a new character on the spot and about to play him and transforming the person standing next to me into the character of Toni coming out in full drag for the first time as it was described in our treatment. Bob's expression tightened and he started breathing heavily through his nostrils, a little detail that would later become his trademark signal for impending rage. Even in the mirror I could see the veins pulsating in his forehead.

Still staring straight into his drink and never once looking at the queen beside me he blurts out,

"You're wearing a dress? A fucking dress? And that hair? And fuckin' make-up? I only hope your father drops dead before he ever sees you like this! You should be ashamed of yourself. Hear me?"

I was still focused on the three shot in the mirror and I must attest to this right here. Though I hold Martin Scorsese in the highest regard, I think anyone could've directed this scene by merely calling "action." In fact, Bob was not only directing himself in an improvisation of an entirely new character, he was also directing this poor insecure crossdresser, forcing her to behave the way the now vulnerable and insecure character 'Toni' would because it was crystal clear that she was the target of Uncle Enzo's rage. And Bob was also directing me, the poor schmuck in the mirror sitting between them. I couldn't help but play my role perfectly: embarrassed, uncomfortable, literally squirming on my stool, just the way a real actor would play an unsuspecting straight patron suddenly caught in the middle of this awkward scene. It was an electrifying and terrifying experience. The drag queen stiffened up and got so flushed her color actually penetrated those thick layers of make-up.

The tension was too much for me to bear. I just felt so bad for the poor guy/gal I couldn't take it anymore, so I broke character and started rambling on apologetically.

"He didn't mean you. He's an actor. He's actually going to be famous soon! Really! You know *The Godfather*? He's playing Brando as a young man. Don Corleone as a young man. He did it already but it hasn't come out yet. Three more months…"

But nothing I could say could undo what just happened. She just yanked her drink away, flashed us a look she probably had directed at many an asshole, then careful not to spill her Shirley Temple, stumbled away on her sky high heels off into the crowd where she immersed herself in the pulsing disco beat.

We slugged down our drinks then Bob casually asked if I needed to take a leak.

"No, I'm good."

"You sure?"

"Yeah. Why, you?"

"No! No… I mean yeah, but I'm fine. I can wait."

"Wait for what? Me?"

I think by my body language he knew my bladder was about to explode also. I glanced over to where Bob was looking. The two rest rooms, labeled "Men" and "Ladies," and with as many transsexuals and transvestites going into the men's room as there were very butch macho dykes going into the ladies room. To the best of my recollection, the conversation went something like this:

ME: "Which one do we use?"

BOB: "Men's room. We gotta, right? It's the law."

ME: "You really wanna go in there? I'll wait outside and you can tell me how it went."

BOB: "Get the fuck..."

ME: "So, what, the ladies room? At least they have stalls."

BOB: "Yeah, we'll wind up in jail."

ME: "How would they know we're really guys? Do they know those guys going in there are really women?"

BOB: "They don't have dicks. We have dicks. Can't take the chance."

ME: Yeah, I guess. I can see the headline, "A couple of dicks."

Then the conversation went quiet and soon the decision was clear.

CUT TO:

EXT. CLUB 82 – NIGHT

Jeff pees on the curb between the bumpers of a parked Buick Roadmaster and a Ford Mustang, while Bob works a spot two car bumpers down.

Little did we know we had just gazed into the future, grappled with, and solved an important societal issue that would arise decades later, the alternative to gender assigned bathrooms, way before it would even be perceived as a problem. We were gender pioneers!

If you're wondering what ever happened to *Pink and Blue*, well, here it is. The experience at Club 82 energized Bob to take the next step and have the great make-up artist Dick Smith make him up as a woman so he'd see what he'd look like before committing himself any further to the project. I wish I had been there to see it but he did it in complete secrecy. In fact Marc Rubin and I learned about it from a blurb leaked to one of the New York newspapers. That's how Bob's agent Harry Ufland found out about it too, not just the make-up session but the project *Pink and Blue* itself. Bob had also been keeping that a secret up to that point.

Ufland went ballistic. No way his potentially hottest client, his soon to be huge movie star client, could be attached to some cockamamie project about his leading man getting a sex change, written by two young unknown and untested talents. Even without DeNiro, noted Producer Ed Pressman snapped up our story through his deal with Twentieth Century Fox and

Adventures of a Subversive Cult Filmmaker from the Golden Age.

we were paid to expand our treatment into a screenplay. But it would die a slow death in that infamous place known as "development hell," while Bob was out shooting his next movie where he'd once again tap into his improvisational genius by asking that simple question, "You talkin' to me?"

The *Pink and Blue* experience energized me to get back to writing. This time I was determined to write an entire screenplay myself. The first thing that came to mind was the idea I abandoned two years before, the one JoAnn dubbed the stupidest thing she ever heard. The one about the worms.

I searched around until I found the yellow legal pad I first sketched out the idea on with title scrawled at the top; *Skworm*! With a fresh eye, the first thing that struck me was the way I spelled Squirm. Skworm. Too cutesy. The idea was weird enough without needing to put a spin on it. So *Squirm* it was. Every night when I returned home from Janus I'd immerse myself in that screenplay with no idea what I'd do with it once it was finished.

12. FROM MADE MAN TO MADMAN

After a late night writing session on *Squirm* I arrived at Janus to learn a man named Stephen Frankfurt had called asking for me. His name was slightly familiar to me as some legendary ad man who was supposed to be the youngest person ever to head a major agency. That's if it was the same guy. But if it was, what could he want from me?

I returned his call and sure enough it was the same guy and he wanted to know if I'd be interested in working on a new project, which was to create a campaign for the new Ken Russell movie adaptation of the Rock opera *Tommy*.

Steve explained he'd seen my short film *The Ringer*, which you'll recall actually vilified advertising and mass marketing, especially to young people, but he thought it also showed I really understood the manipulative secrets of the trade. Talk about irony. Steve had formed his own branch of the major agency Kenyon and Eckhardt. It was called Frankfurt communications and it specialized in movie advertising for big studio releases. Iconic campaigns like "Pray for Rosemary's Baby" and the Alien's "In space, no one can hear you scream" established his company as the go-to advertising and marketing shop for high profile studio movies. He was just looking for concepts, so I figured why not? It shouldn't take up much of my time and the extra money will ad a little more cushion to the family nest. He invited me to a screening of the rough cut.

I naively thought I was the only one who Steve asked to work on the Tommy campaign, but when I arrived at the Columbia Pictures screening room I found out otherwise. Turned out Steve was known for bringing in New York creative people of all stripes, so there I was taking a seat along the likes

Adventures of a Subversive Cult Filmmaker from the Golden Age.

of Milton Glazer, Andy Warhol and who knows who else. By the way, seeing Andy Warhol anywhere in New York City back in the 70s was no big deal. One reason was that he popped up everywhere. The other is, like so many other iconic artists, he didn't reach his top echelon fame and appreciation until after his death so when I took a seat near him there was no 'holy shit, Andy Warhol!' element. In fact, I would've been way more freaked out that Milton Glazer was one of them but didn't know what he looked like.

After the screening it was off to the conference room where Steve gave us a general pep talk and set us each off to come up with something. I guessed he threw me in the mix primarily because of my age. After all, *Tommy* was a huge rock album hit and he wanted to grab the same audience. Pitted against these heavyweights I figured there was no way he'd use anything I did, but he did guarantee me three thousand bucks, (only a grand less than I was paid for writing and directing The Ringer) whether he used anything or not so I had nothing to lose and gave it my best shot.

That night, with the movie still fresh in my mind, I dug out ye ole yellow legal pad I'd been writing Squirm on, flipped to the first fresh blank page and wrote the word "Tommy" on top. Then I dug out my vinyl LP of *Tommy*, set it on the turntable, put on my Mickey Mouse ear headphones and listened with my trusty Bic pen at the ready. As soon as I heard the lyrics, "That deaf dumb and blind kid sure plays a mean pinball," it triggered an image from the movie of Roger Daltry with his eyes and ears covered in black along with a black cork in his mouth. Great image for the movie. But I was getting ahead of myself. Everyone knew *Tommy* the rock opera and best selling album. But they needed to know it was now a movie. Pretty basic communication. So I wrote down the word "Movie" Right beside the word "Tommy," only this time I put a period after *Tommy*. So now I had sort of a clunky statement of cold facts I needed to communicate somehow. 'Tommy. Movie. Okay, back to that image. Why was it so exemplary of the movie? Because it showed the character Tommy with all his senses blocked out, which of course somehow resulted in some super power.

McLuhan claimed all advertising is good news. "Act now and you'll save twenty percent!" "You don't have to be Jewish to eat Levy's Jewish rye!" "There's double action in Baboo!" "Visine gets the red out!" Ads always made some good news claim to lure the suckers to part with their money. So what good news claim could come from seeing this movie? It needed to be a claim that involved the senses. And just like that it came to me, "Your senses will never be the same!" That's quite a claim, but it felt perfect for the drug generation.

Jeff Lieberman • Day Of The Living Me!

So I scribbled out a picture of Daltry with his eyes blocked out by round black glasses, a black cork in his mouth and earphones covering his ears, just like in the movie. Then I wrote my bare bones information lines right under it; "*Tommy*. Movie. Your senses will never be the same."

That didn't sound right. So I changed it to 'the' movie. That was it. "*Tommy*. The Movie. Your senses will never be the same." I shut the record only about twenty minutes in, then fleshed out the rest of the ad campaign. It felt right to stick to that dry, statement of fact thing I had set in motion. So I tried it on the cast. "Elton John is the Pinball Wizard." "Tina Turner is the Acid Queen. "Anne Margret is Nora" and so on, each time ending with the lines, '*Tommy*. The movie. Your senses will never be the same.'

Next day I called Steve's office to set an appointment. He was very surprised I took so little time. He looked over the sheets torn from my yellow legal pad and nodded his approval. Then to my surprise he said, 'What else?'

What else? There was no else. This was all I had. He explained that in advertising you present various different ways to go. But I wasn't an advertising man and didn't want to be. Why show him something that I don't like? This was the way I'd do it. He seemed very disappointed I did so little work on it as he showed me to the door. In fact, I got the feeling he'd be holding back my check. So much for my short stint in advertising.

The next week I was in the Janus editing room and someone had a radio tuned to WNEW, New York's top FM rock station. Suddenly famed disc jockey Scott Muni came on delivering a commercial in his signature raspy voice over the soundtrack to *Tommy*.

"Tina Turner is the Acid Queen, Elton John is the Pinball Wizard'
'*Tommy*. The Movie. You're senses will never be the same!"

My entire campaign, word for word. No copy changes, broadcast over the airwaves! Here I was thinking what I did was a total misfire and it was anything but. I called Steve to ask how that happened so fast. He said that Robert Stigwood, the movie's producer, loved a rough audio test they did with Scott Muni so much he insisted on putting it on the air the way it was. Obviously my one submission beat out all the others. Very strange way to find that out.

Those two sheets of yellow legal pad paper turned out to be pretty much the entire campaign, centered around those simple phrases, "*Tommy*. The Movie. Your senses will never be the same," along with the suggestion of using that iconic image of Roger Daltry with the cork in his mouth and blackened glasses, both of which are now synonymous with the movie. The cast was handled in the exact way I suggested also. The only change was a

Adventures of a Subversive Cult Filmmaker from the Golden Age.

graphic design choice of the great designer Phil Gips who worked with Steve. Phil added another upside-down identical image of Daltry to create sort of Rorschach effect and definitely made it more graphically striking. Though I was never told the reason, but I'm guessing it was a contractual thing, Phil had to use a model instead of Roger Daltry for that photo.

This became the movie poster one sheet, the print ads, radio, everything, even tee shirts and lunch boxes later on. *Tommy* was released by Columbia Pictures and was a huge success. And yeah, I got my paycheck but in advertising, freelancers don't get credited for their work and Phil Gips is associated with creating the poster and Frankfurt the overall campaign. No mention of me at all. Just like with my re-write of *Who Killed Mary Whats'ername*, I was a ghost.

One thing I knew, since I was the only writer on *Squirm*, and hopefully would be the only director, there was no way I wouldn't be credited for my work. If it ever got made…

13. THE HOUSE THAT SQUIRM BUILT

I had just written the words 'The End' on the last page of my *Squirm* script when JoAnn told me George Manasse was on the phone. I don't believe in fate. Nor kismet. Nor the stars lining up just right for something to happen. Nor that anything is "meant to be," or happens for some cosmic purpose. But my lack of faith was about to be put to the test.

I hadn't spoken to George since *Mary Whats'ername* so hearing from him was a surprise in itself. But the fact that George just happened to be looking for a low budget B- horror movie script took the word coincidence to a whole other level.

George was working with two successful Broadway producers who were dipping their toes into producing movies and were looking for something they could do right away that could be ready for the next Cannes Film Festival seven months off.

When I told him about *Squirm* he said it sounded exactly like what they were looking for. He met me downtown to get a copy of the script and read it right away. He loved it and immediately passed it on to the producers and one day later I was in their offices at 1650 Broadway.

Their names were Edgar Lansbury (brother of Angela) and Joseph Beruh and they were riding high with two hit Broadway musicals, *Godspell* and *The Magic Show*. So if they settled on a movie project, the financing would come from them along with their theater investment group. After an amiable meeting with me they screened my short film *The Ringer* and one day later I had a writer-director deal with a plan to start pre-production immediately for a late fall shoot. I was given a tiny office and commuted to the city daily on the Long Island Railroad, but sometimes I would drive in and

Adventures of a Subversive Cult Filmmaker from the Golden Age.

park at the public lot on 54th street between 8th and Broadway, right next to an empty CBS studio space which was in the early demolition stages of being converted into a nightclub which would be called Studio 54. I crossed Broadway then headed down to 51st and the Lansbury/Beruh offices at 1650 Broadway which was a show business landmark filled with composers, playwrights, writers and producers.

Right down the hall from Lansbury/Beruh was the office of producer Howard Gottfried and his partner, the famed playwright and screenwriter Paddy Chayevsky. The duo had just produced the movie *The Hospital* starring George C. Scott and were in the early stages of another project called *Altered States* to be directed by Ken Russel, the director of *Tommy*.

It was a very free-flowing creative atmosphere in the Lansbury/Beruh suites with Howard or Paddy frequently entering Edgar's spacious office and just plopping down on the coach next to the baby grand piano to schmooze. Playwrights Israel Horowitz and Murray Schiskal would call Joe Beruh almost daily and they'd invariably wind up yelling at each other until one of them hung up on the other.

Paul Schaffer had already been the musical director of their production of *Godspell* in Toronto and had now moved to New York to do the same on *The Magic Show*. Though Paul was a frequent fixture in the offices, it wasn't until decades later we'd really get to know each other.

Edgar's sister Angela would drop by on occasion too, which was always a pure delight. Then there was Ulu Grosbard, who had directed the play *View from the Bridge* for Edgar and Joe and was prepping a movie to star Dustin Hoffman called *Straight Time*. Ulu would occasionally drop by my tiny office to chat and over time I'd glean more wisdom about actors and directing from him than I could've learned at any film school. One little gem was that an actor can't convincingly play a character that's much smarter than they are. He actually named a certain well-known actor to prove his point.

This was the big time all right and I was in so far over my head I had no choice but to just depend on my wits, and whatever natural talent that others saw in me and just fake it. Guess that's where the cliché "fake it til you make it" comes from.

Speaking of faking it, now that I actually sold my movie, the stupidity of the central idea JoAnn reacted to suddenly consumed me. A movie about worms taking over a town? Worms? What's scary about worms? Icky and slimy yes, but scary and threatening? These serious successful Broadway producers actually wanted to make this cockamamie idea into a movie? Did they see something I didn't see or did I somehow disguise this central problem with good story structure and likable characters? What if I can't make worms scary? The entire movie would fall apart. And they'd only find out when it was way too late to do anything about it. What had I gotten myself into?

I selected the salt-water species Glycera found around the eastern seacoasts for my script because they had big black pinchers and actually did bite. But how would they look blown up on a movie screen? Would they transform into the stuff of nightmares the way giant ants and spiders did in those matinee radiation movies of my youth? I had to see for myself.

I bought a box of Glycera or "bloodworms" as the fishermen called them, then placed them all over one of my daughter's doll's body. For added horror effect I plucked out one of the eyeballs and draped a worm inside of it so it would hang out of the socket as if it had eaten her brain.

I grabbed my El Cheapo 8-millimeter home movie camera and filmed it, moving in as close to the worms as I could and prodding them with a pencil to open their mouths and display those nasty sharp black fangs. On a second roll I shot just worm close ups from every angle, shifting the lighting to make them seem monstrous with no sense of scale.

I took the two rolls to the local drugstore for developing and was told I'd get a call when they were ready. I waited impatiently until they finally called four days later to report that the film was ready for pick up. I retrieved the rolls then set up my 8mm projector in the living room. JoAnn and I shut all the blinds to make the apartment dark as possible. The stakes couldn't be higher for me because if I wasn't confident I could make these worms scary, how could I expect the movie to work? I flipped the projector switch and what came on was a horror all right, some little girl's birthday party! Instead of worms, there was a typical family gathering, parents, aunts and uncles, all surrounding their little birthday girl watching her blow out the candles.

The drugstore had mislabeled one of my film rolls and I got someone else's home movie, which meant they got mine!

I turned to JoAnn and we both cracked up. It was possible that at that very moment, the poor family on the screen were seeing bloody slimy worms crawling in and out of a doll's eyeball instead of their little angel's birthday party!

Fortunately, the other roll was mine and the worms looked fantastic, even in 8-millimeter. Glistening and slimy, when they opened those grotesque mouths, you could almost hear the sounds they emitted, screams that I'd later dub in with the sounds of pigs being slaughtered to transform them into electrified monsters.

Adventures of a Subversive Cult Filmmaker from the Golden Age.

When I returned to the drugstore the poor family who got the wrong film had already returned it and I turned over the birthday film in an even swap. I didn't ask if the people said anything when they turned it in but I did derive some pleasure in knowing that in all likelihood, *Squirm* had already grossed out its first audience. Now I just hoped I could do the same to the masses.

Casting. Something I knew little or nothing about since my only previous casting experience was on *The Ringer*. Now I'd be working with veteran producers and an actual casting agent. The first piece of business was to find the three leads, starting with the leading man, Mick, a New Yorker type in his mid or late 20s who takes a bus down to the fictional Georgia town of Fly Creek to visit a girl he met at an antique fair in New York. Lansbury and Beruh suggested an actor named Martin Sheen who they'd given his big break to in a play they produced called The Subject was Roses. Martin came up to the office and although he looked very young for his age, he was clearly at least five years older than what I was looking for. But then again, movies cheat on real age all the time so I looked past that and gave my blessings to casting him based on Edgar and Joe's confidence in him.

Now that Martin had the role, he called and told me he was appearing in a production of *Death of a Salesman* starring George C. Scott at Circle in the Square and arranged for me to see the play, then meet with him afterwards at the bar.

Meanwhile, word had spread to all my New York friends that I was actually making a real movie, the first, and only among my fellow film school graduates to do so. I got a call from a fellow named John Poole who had headed the 16mm division while I was at Janus. John asked if I could do him a favor and see a gym buddy of his for the role of Roger, the son of a worm farmer who has a life long crush on his neighbor Geri, the girl that Mick is coming down from New York to visit.

John's actor friend's name was Sylvester Stallone, and he was working as a waiter to support his young family while waiting for some boxing movie he wrote to get financing. I had seen Stallone in a low budget movie called *Sexual Freedom in Brooklyn* (later changed to *The Lords of Flatbush*) and he made a great impression on me. But Roger was one of the three main leads in *Squirm* and there was no way I could buy Stallone as a Southern bumpkin and didn't want to give him false hopes so I just had to say he wasn't right for it, but I did like his work.

I picked up my house seat ticket at the Circle in the Square will-call window and settled in to watch George C. Scott's memorable rendition of

Jeff Lieberman • Day Of The Living Me!

Willy Lohman, then retired to the bar to wait for Martin to get out of make-up. He arrived with George who ordered up drinks all around, then after some small talk, George picked up his drink and declared in that commanding voice of his,

"Okay gentlemen, you have some business to attend to, I'll afford you some privacy."

He shook my hand and took his drink over to a table, then Martin turned his full attention to me.

"Jeff, I was wondering what Mick does for a living."

I was taken aback. I had no idea what my fictional character did other than his actions the story. I had never even heard the term "back story," let alone thought about making him a three dimensional character. I only knew the plot so that's how I answered him.

"He comes down from New York to visit his girlfriend."

"I know, but in New York. Actor's studio. Could he be an actor?"

I thought about it and didn't see how that could negatively affect the movie so I said "Sure."

"Great!, said Martin as he sat up in his chair. "In that scene where he holds up the skull in the dentist office after he identifies the victim, can he say "Alas poor Yorick, I knew him well?"

Uh-oh. This could be a problem.

The next morning Edgar and Joe asked me how my meeting went with Martin. I told them that since they're giving me five weeks to shoot the movie and one of those weeks will be just shooting special effects scenes with worms, I can't take time with one of my actors trying to work in Shakespeare. They were very understanding and took care of breaking the news to Martin.

We also needed a young leading lady which I'd learn were called 'ingénues' in casting circles. Attractive young actresses are legion in both L.A. and New York. But you're more likely to find trained ones with theater experience in NY than you are in tinsel town. And since Edgar and Joe produced *Godspell*, they had a deep bench of actresses who had appeared in various productions of the show, (like Gilda Radner) both in Toronto and New York. Toward the end of a long day the last ingénue on the list entered the office. She was head and shoulders over all the others in the looks department. Tall, blonde and naturally sexy. On her resume it said she was a Ford model which didn't surprise us. Edgar and Joe just gawked at her beauty so I broke the ice and asked her the routine questions. Turns out she was from Georgia and though she'd trained to erase her southern accent, she could easily revert to it for the role. I finally got to the question we had to ask all of them up front. Since this was a horror movie, the genre called for at least one nudity scene, which at that time only meant someone showing bare breasts. Frontal nudity was strictly forbidden.

She shrugged and said with that slight drawl,

"I have no problem with my body."

The way she said it made us all melt. We just sat there gawking at her, which (justifiably) made her uncomfortable. Finally Joe wrapped it up, checking back at her resume.

"Okay Miss Bassinger."

"Call me Kim."'

"Alright, Kim. Thanks for coming in, we'll let you know."

We watched her every move as she rose from the chair, shook all our hands and sauntered out the door.

Now it was Edgar's turn.

"Well Lieberman, what do you think?"

"Who's gonna believe she lives next door to a worm farm? It'd be like Little Abner and Daisy Mae, a cartoon."

Edgar and Joe were theatre people and first and foremost respectful of the playwright, or in this case the screenwriter. I was the *auteur* in the vernacular of that time. So they deferred to my opinion and crossed off Kim Bassinger's name.

Over the years I'd often fantasize what would occur had the older, wizened me sat in on that initial casting session, listening to this cocky young auteur explain why this most incredible looking young southern lady was not right for the role. I'd picture myself grabbing that 25 year old me by the collar and shoving him up against the nearest wall, then yelling in his ear.

Schmuck! What's the name of this movie?"

"Uh... Squii..."

"And what's it about? Worms! Invading a small town. So who's the audience for this? Teenagers, mostly of the male variety. And who do you think they'd want to see naked in a shower?"

"Kim... Baaa…"

"You think they give a crap about how realistic it would be that she'd live next door to a worm farm? Are worms being super charged by an electrical storm and attacking and eating people *realistic*?"

The younger me would only shake his head feebly.

"Exactly!"

Jeff Lieberman • Day Of The Living Me!

But sadly, in order to become that older me I had to make knuckle headed mistakes like that one.

The production itself was fraught with the usual near disasters common in shooting low budget movies chock full of special effects. Even so, our special effects make-up man, the young Rick Baker, enabled me to sell the idea that electrified worms could burrow deep into human flesh, as exemplified in the now iconic scene of Roger's face being consumed right before our eyes.

And it was just that scene that sold the head of marketing at Columbia Pictures on picking up the North American rights to the movie. Terms were quickly negotiated and it looked like I scored a studio release on my first try. Pretty cool I thought. But as a formality the head of the studio at the time, David Beagleman, was obliged to sign off on the purchase. As luck would have it, or rather bad luck, Beagleman scheduled his private screening the night of a previously planned dinner engagement and since the studio was on the way to the restaurant, he brought his wife Gladys along to avoid having to make two trips.

The next day Edgar and Joe got the bad news that the studio had decided to pass on the movie, with curt instructions to come and pick up the print. No further explanation. But when Edgar and Joe came to get the print from the screening room, the projectionist who screened it for the Beaglemans told them what happened.

Gladys arrived decked out in a full-length mink and was constantly checking her watch as the lights went down, way more concerned about being late for their dinner date than watching a movie about disgusting worms taking over a southern town. But her disgust turned to utter revulsion when the close-up of worms crawling up Roger's face filled the screen. She stood up and yelled at David.

"If you have anything to do with this garbage I want a divorce! I mean it!"

David signaled to the projectionist to turn up the lights and they were out of there in a flash. So the same scene that excited his sales department buried our chances of a major studio release. Or so it seemed.

Undiscouraged, Edgar and Joe took the movie to the Cannes festival and it was the hit of the film market place. Legendary mogul Sam Arkoff, much more adept at B-movie horror, loved the picture and bought world rights for his company American International Pictures, (A.I.P). He advanced Lansbury and Beruh the total amount it took to make the movie, which meant profits for all investors were virtually assured which would also include

Adventures of a Subversive Cult Filmmaker from the Golden Age.

my twelve percent ownership stake.

Just like that I had a movie that would play all over the world and it only took twelve months from the time I finished the script to the time it'd premiere in American theaters, an event that would provide my next learning experience.

It was July of '76, a Friday, and opening night of *"Squirm"* in 55 theaters in New York city and the surrounding suburbs. I led JoAnn and a group of close friends to midtown where we chose the biggest theater playing the movie, the RKO twin on Broadway, just north of 42nd street in Times Square. This was the early days of the multiplex concept when theater chains started to break their existing theaters up into two and sometimes three separate theaters by merely erecting walls right up and down the seating isles. These were just sheet rock thin walls so if you were unlucky enough to get a seat next to one, you could hear the soundtrack from the movie next door almost as loud as the movie you were trying to watch.

The RKO Times square was huge, one of the grand old movie palaces like the nearby Roxy or Paramount, so even cut it in half, each theater held upwards of 900 people.

We bought our tickets and all got a kick out of the lobby cards displayed in the windows depicting various scenes from the movie. But as we entered another giant lobby poster caught my eye, 'Coming soon, Dino De Laurentiis's *King Kong*! Great, what a buzz kill. On my big night I had to be reminded of how Dino killed two of my brilliant concoctions? Of course he didn't know that but fuck him anyway. I hoped the movie bombed. (which it did)

By the time we took our seats about twenty rows back from the screen, the theater was sold out. SOLD OUT!

It was a very racially mixed audience, more than half black and Hispanic. And carrying an R-rating meant it was comprised of all adults. It's important to note there was no such thing as test screenings back then for small independent horror movies. Or if there was, Squirm certainly never had one. So this was the first time I'd be seeing the movie with an audience. When I got done surveying the the late comers scrambling for seats, I noticed the A.I.P. logo was being projected faintly on the heavy velvet closed red curtains. Forgetting my surroundings, I started shouting.

"Wait! What are they doing? They're starting the movie with the curtain closed and the lights on and people are still finding their seats!"

The crawl at the beginning, my tongue in cheek prologue that set the story up with the crazy claim that what the audience was about to see was a true story, was totally lost on the curtain. *Nobody*, not one person among nine hundred was reading it!

I shot out of my seat and started for the projectionist's booth. But JoAnn stopped me and hit me with some cold reality. First of all, there was no way anyone was going to allow me into the projection booth and even if they did, there was not a chance in hell that any projectionist was going to stop a movie, rewind it, then start it again when some schmuck from the audience deemed it the right time. Even if the schmuck happened to be the director. This was not some private screening. And neither was the over fifty other eight o' clock shows around the New York metro area!

For all I knew every one of them were playing the movie over their own curtains also! I sunk back in my seat in a cold sweat. At that very moment I realized I had to let it go. From my log line on that yellow pad, to the RKO twin in Times Square New York, my creation, my baby, was now out there on its own to sink or swim. And there was nothing I could do about it.

Welcome to show biz kid.

Soon after, when *Rocky* exploded making Sylvester Stallone a huge star, then later on *9 ½ Weeks* put Kim Bassinger right up front in the public eye as the new Hollywood sex symbol, and then *Apocalypse Now* launched Martin Sheen into stardom, I could only speculate on what casting all three of them would've done for *Squirm* in future TV and video sales. And for me.

The movie's done very well over the years, better than 95 percent of the low budget horror cranked out back in that so-called Golden Age of the genre, but it's gained its "evergreen" status with the 'no-name,' but excellent cast of Don Scardino, Patricia Pearcy and R.A. Dow.

I try not to dwell on what casting those stars-to-be would've done for my career, but no doubt it would've made me look like some casting genius. A spotter of talent, a star maker even! Alas, I was none of those things. In any case, my share of Squirm bought us our first house in Westchester New York. We christened it the house that *Squirm* built.

I wasn't trying to make any sort of social or political comment with Squirm. At least not consciously. However, soon after the movie's release, critics found some very profound subtext, which I myself wasn't aware of. Nature getting revenge on man for his disrespect of ecology. The symbolism of man's mortality and his inevitable fate of becoming worm food. Even themes of suppressed sexuality in the main characters. This could all very well be true, but if it is, it wasn't intentional on my part.

Adventures of a Subversive Cult Filmmaker from the Golden Age.

Director of photography Joseph Mangine lining up a shot for *Squirm*, while I practice my director's look and Assistant cameraman Chris Balton sneaks a cigarette.

Don Scardino playing the role of 'Mick' while I play the role of his director.

R.A. Dow as 'Roger' submerged in (artificial) worms!

With Squirm producer Edgar Lansbury in his office at 1560 Broadway, New York City.

Jeff Lieberman • Day Of The Living Me!

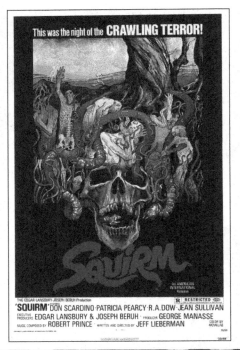

Iconic one sheet poster by legendary artist Drew Struzan.

Actual production clapper slate used in the shooting of *Squirm*.

Squirm playing on 42nd. Street, double billed with *Tentacles*, 1976

14. TRIPPING ON BLUE SUNSHINE

Since Squirm recouped its entire investment before it even hit the screens, Lansbury and Beruh were keen on rolling the dice on me again. Now that I'd been through the grinding ordeal of making an independent movie, I needed an idea that was worthy of the commitment to do it all again.

No more working from my living room couch. I now had a home office all to myself where I could just close the door and dive back into my creative zone.

My thoughts drifted back to 'The Ringer' and the whole subject of drugs and once again how the government used their misinformation propaganda machine in the 60's and 70's in a similar way to their atomic bomb scares of the 50s. I pondered how these new scares affected so many of my generation as they entered adulthood. And how once again, Uncle Sam managed to scare the living shit out of me personally...

FLASH BACK TO 1972. JoAnn was pregnant and she learned about this new thing called the Lamaze natural childbirth method. Giving birth without being knocked out on drugs like civilizations have done since the dawn of man. I knew that in other countries - especially third world countries like Vietnam; it was common practice for peasants to just wade into the reeds, give birth, then go back to picking rice. But here in America we've evolved to a standard practice of hospitalization and anesthesia, which virtually removed the mother from the birthing experience.

Baby boomers had learned to question just about everything the previous generation did, and I mean everything, right across the board. The new credo was to take nothing for granted to be true just because our parents, or their generation claimed it was true. So when the boomers entered adulthood and were confronted with the prospect of having a child, the whole process of reproduction was ripe for re-examination, or "re-visiting," a term that sprouted up around that time.

A revisit of childbirth would require taking it back to, well, its inception, which was giving birth naturally. No drugs of any kind. The mother would be awake and aware through the entire process.

Since this was the early 1970's when the women's liberation movement was kicking into high gear, the question of the male role in the birthing process had to be revisited too. The tradition of dad pacing nervously in the waiting room until the doctor came out and declared "it's a boy" or "it's girl" was just not gonna cut it in the age of Aquarius.

The new thinking was, since the father was an equal partner in the parenting endeavor, he should fill an important role in the process of childbirth. "Process" was another word that suddenly worked its way into every day discourse right around then.

So the husband's role was to be right there at the mother's side through the whole thing, making it a team effort.

JoAnn tried to sell me on this Lamaze technique idea. I said fine, if she wants to go through the pain, that's her call, but I'm not going to any classes. It was pointless to me. I learned all I needed to know from Cowboy movies and endless episodes of *Gun Smoke*. The water breaks, the woman starts screaming in pain and the nervous husband is sent out to fetch hot water. But I assured her that if she's actually going to be awake through it all, I'll be at her side the whole time holding her hand. But classes? No way.

Six months later her water broke and she told me very calmly we needed to go to the hospital. I immediately freaked out. I mean, I went into an instant state of utter panic. I ran out to the car, then realizing I left her behind, ran back and got her and put her in the car. Then I got behind the wheel and realized I had no keys. I ran back to the apartment to snatch them, this time remembering to lock the door. When I got back into the car JoAnn was breathing really weirdly, short quick breathes, nothing like normal breathing. She explained she was breathing to the tune of *Yankee Doodle*.

"This is what they taught you?" She nodded while she kept it up.

"What's Yankee Doodle got to do with having a baby?!"

I wove my way through traffic into the city, then steered up to the curb at Flower Fifth Avenue Hospital and escorted JoAnn up to the maternity area while she Yankee Doodled all the way. My brother Gary's love of science led him to a career in medicine and he was coincidentally interning at this very

Adventures of a Subversive Cult Filmmaker from the Golden Age.

hospital. In fact he was somewhere in the building on rounds. My parents were already there in the waiting room, my dad brimming with excitement while my mother locked into her usual state of near dread of what could go wrong.

I hung with them until a nurse came out and summoned me to the pre-delivery room. Pre-delivery room? What's that, an on deck circle where you wait for a nurse to open a door and yell "next"? Had I attended the classes I'd have known exactly what to expect and that it was the place mothers to be were taken to await full dilation. As I entered the room, the whole experience was about to morph into a living horror movie. There was JoAnn, lying on a gurney with both feet propped up in support stirrups. The nurse guided me to a view between her legs and said, "Look daddy? What a beautiful baby!"

Beautiful baby? What the hell was she talking about?! All I saw was this purplish egg shaped thing sticking out of JoAnn's vagina! It was all wet and matted with black feathery hairs! I had witnessed sparrows cracking out of eggs when I was a kid and that's exactly what this looked like. Only this was supposed to be a human baby, not a genetically mutated bird! Then it hit me. All those government warnings about LSD causing genetic damage resonated in my brain. What if they were right and acid DID cause genetic damage? Holy shit! I was looking right at it, the worst case of genetic damage in the history of evolution: a human bird!

I tried my best not to reveal my sheer panic to JoAnn or she'd freak out too, which is what I figured the nurse was doing too, pretending to be seeing a beautiful baby while she was actually seeing the same grotesque monstrosity I was. I forced myself to form a smile.

"Yeah Jo, it's beautiful, fantastic."

I kissed JoAnn on the cheek then left the room with my mind racing to figure out what to say to my parents. How do I break the news to them? "Mom, dad, I took LSD. And because of that we're having a bird. But it's a *healthy* bird and we'll take care of it as if it were human."

But when I finally mustered up the courage to approach them, I couldn't say anything. I just slumped in my seat in a stupor, shuddering at what would soon occur in the delivery room. I knew I promised to hold JoAnn's hand during the whole thing but I just couldn't muster up the nerve. When my brother came by, I told him I decided not to go in there, making up some excuse about staying with our parents.

About a half hour later, these two big orderly guys in green scrubs swooped in and grabbed me like I was some kind of mental patient (which in a

Jeff Lieberman • Day Of The Living Me!

way, I probably should have been.) My brother put them up to it to get me into the delivery room no matter what. Firmly grasping both my elbows on either side, they hustled me to the entrance just as JoAnn was arriving on her gurney, breathing out Yankee Doodle like she was backing up James Cagney.

When the orderlies deposited me in the delivery room, my knees were so wobbly I had to grab onto a nearby sink to steady myself. JoAnn's breathing got faster and faster with each contraction. Blood drained from my face and the whole room started spinning.

I braced myself for the sight of the doctor pulling out that big hairy half human half bird, wings flapping like a chicken at a kosher butcher shop and screaming like the Pterodactyl in the 50's sci-fi movie Rodan. BWAAAA!

But the "bwaaa" came out as a "whaaaa! WHAAAA!" eminating from the mouth of a perfectly formed all human baby. A girl, complete with every anatomical part perfectly formed and in place down to the last detail. She even had cuticles!

FLASH FORWARD back to my home office as I jotted down the words, "What if LSD chromosome damage was real!" The fact that it was so real to me, that I actually *believed* JoAnn was giving birth to a human bird was tantamount to my believing I was shrinking back when I was ten years old. What if I wasn't the only one? Millions of my generation had experimented with LSD during the late 60s into the 70s. Deep down they all must harbor a fear there could be some validity to the detrimental long-term effects of this mysterious drug. Why not tap into that universal fear the way Hollywood tapped into our generation's fear of the atomic bomb back in the fifties? What if there was a particular strain of LSD that altered our chromosomes the way they claimed radiation did?

Since the accepted after effects of LSD were flashbacks occurring weeks or even months after taking the drug, what if, instead of flashbacks, a certain strain of acid triggered a genetic mutation that turned a person into a human time bomb of unfettered violence? And of course, this drug would kick in just when the baby boomers who ingested it back, say, ten years ago in 1967, were now becoming the establishment and having children of their own like I did, buying houses and settling into family lives very similar to the lives their parents lived, the ones they so vehemently rejected.

I dropped my yellow pad and headed downstairs where JoAnn was preparing a roast.

"I have an idea for my next movie!"

"Can it wait? I'm cooking dinner."

96

Adventures of a Subversive Cult Filmmaker from the Golden Age.

"What, you don't want to hear it?"

"I do. But it's better if you just write it. I already proved I know nothing about movies."

I went back upstairs and dove right into it. First thing I needed was a title, which I knew should be the name of the LSD that caused this to happen. I wrote down all the names of acid, 'Blue Cheer,' 'Owsley Purple,' 'Orange Sunshine.' Then I mixed the words around to make up a fictional strain, but also serve as a cool sounding movie title. I finally arrived at *Blue Sunshine*, then flipped to a new page and wrote that title again at the top, then started writing the screenplay in longhand. JoAnn would soon learn what the idea was because she was still my personal typist.

The plot centered around a specific batch of LSD that was sold around the Stanford University campus in 1967. The movie took place ten years later when those who did the drug back then were now upstanding citizens including among them a doctor, a police officer and a congressional candidate. Though totally unaware, each of the *Blue Sunshine* recipients was a walking time bomb ready to transform into psychopathic killers.

In the midst of all this, my father suddenly suffered a fatal heart attack at the age of fifty-five. I was devastated and literally couldn't function. I expressed my grief with anger, lashing out at everyone around me, JoAnn included.

Blue Sunshine was budgeted at three million dollars which included shooting on the streets and subways of New York and flash backs to the 1960's college campus scene. But I couldn't wait for the producers to find that much money, I needed to immerse myself in work right then and there or I'd go insane. So Edgar and Joe agreed to finance it themselves for a fraction of the cost, a half million dollars, which necessitated cutting out all the 1960's flashbacks. It also meant we needed to shoot the movie in Los Angeles because New York City and its subways were way beyond our financial reach. Three months later we were in pre- production in Los Angles, with George Manasse, my line producer on *Squirm*, serving as producer.

With *Blue Sunshine*, I had enough confidence to consciously meld my political and social commentary on the world around me into a movie. The phenomenon of my generation, the so called "baby boomers," making our transition from carefree hippies with our change-the-world idealism, entering into that dreaded Real World we always tried to tuck back into the furthest recesses of our brains, seemed ripe for social commentary. Suddenly attitudes toward the career world, the job world, the family world, all the things we spent our late teens and early twenties rebelling against, were morphing into our own reality. But at what cost? Could we make this total transition unscathed? I knew we'd have to pay the piper in various ways, but I needed something symbolic to represent what that penalty for our youthful indiscretions might be. By tapping into the fear the government tried so pathetically to instill in us about the horrors of LSD, I used that same pre-sold fear to fuel my story, which was set around the end of this awkward and largely hypocritical generational transition into the new establishment. I also saw in it the opportunity to comment on the politics and fashions of that post hippie time, as well as the profound musical transition that was about to take place from rock 'n roll to disco.

I also wrote the ad campaign line for the publicists, aimed at triggering the paranoia of my target audience:

"Did you ever hear the words Blue Sunshine? Try to remember. Your life may depend on it."

How's that for a scare campaign?

15. MARTINIS WITH GOD

While I was prepping *Blue Sunshine*, Steve Frankfurt invited me to join him for breakfast at the Polo Lounge at the Beverly Hills Hotel to discuss a new project. Robert Stigwood had adapted another hit record into a movie, this time the Beatles iconic *Sgt. Peppers Lonely Hearts Club Band.* I explained to Steve that now that I'm shooting my second movie, I really wanted to focus on that, not advertising other people's movies. But Steve was a great guy, funny, extremely talented and we were forming a friendship, so I offered to attend an L.A. rough-cut screening just to give him my two cents.

Unlike the *Tommy* rough cut, this thing was God awful, a top to bottom misfire. In fact, I had no idea what the storyline was, just a cavalcade of stars of the times, along with Stigwood super stars The Bee Gees singing Beatle songs from that landmark album. My verdict was that no amount of clever advertising was going to save this turkey. Steve surprisingly agreed and offered that Robert Stigwood himself felt the same way about the incoherence of the narrative. In a desperate attempt to fix it, Stigwood decided to have someone narrate the whole thing, virtually explaining what was supposedly going on as it unfolded. In order to make it seem like this was planned to begin with, Stigwood decided to put this narrator on camera in the character of 'Mr. Kite,' who was mentioned in the Beatles song, and have him tell the story which of course would require further shooting on the sound stage sets created for the movie.

It was the celebrity they chose for this role that turned me around; the one and only George Burns. George had a huge career resurgence with his Oscar winning performance in *The Sunshine Boys* and then lead role in the recent hit movie *Oh God*. I was curious to see *Sgt. Pepper* again with

George's pieces cut in, playing the character of Mr. Kite as sort of a town square barker rendition of a narrator. With his addition, the movie became if not bearable, at least coherent.

My taking on the job had very little to do with money, and less to do with any ambitions I had in advertising because I had none. It had all to do with George Burns himself and I wanted to meet him. I actually made that a condition of our agreement. Here's how. It seemed a young lady working for Steve I'll call Katy, was "dating" George. I put quote marks around the word dating because she was around 34 and George was 81, so I just assumed sex was off the table. Or certainly not on a table. Or as George would put it, "Sex at my age is like trying to shoot pool with a rope."

But I didn't want to just meet George. I was never the type to eagerly shake a celebrities hand and tell them what a big fan I was. That's the kind of bullshit they deal with everywhere they go. And now that he was hot again from his hit movie *Oh God*, I figured the onslaught had to be ten times worse.

I wanted to hang with him. Not as a fan and celebrity but as sort of equals in a just guys hanging out way. So I devised a plan. Next time Katy was in L.A. and had a date set up with George, she was to tell him that she had a friend she wanted to double date with. Then I'd come along as the friend's date. A variation on the beard concept.

It didn't take long for the double date of a lifetime to be set up for a Saturday night, starting at George's house on Maple Drive in Beverly Hills. I picked up my beard date in the white Chevy rented for me by the *Blue Sunshine* production, then headed over to Maple Drive in the flats of Beverly Hills. Now before you start thinking Ms. Beard was being some great sport for going along with this scheme you need to know that Katy had assured her I was married and wouldn't be putting any moves on her, and she wanted to meet George Burns in the worst way also, so we were equal partners in the ruse.

As we pulled up to the curb at George's address, I shut the engine and just gazed at the house. Katy had told me this was the house that George lived in for decades with Gracie and where they raised their son Ronnie. It looked so familiar I assumed it was the house the studio modeled the set from for the *George Burns and Gracie Allen TV Show*.

Following in the footsteps of Harry Von Zel from that show, I walked up to the front door and rang the doorbell. Suddenly a weird thing happened. My heart started pounding like Ola-fucking-tunji. All my nonchalance regarding celebrities evaporated. I could not believe I was actually doing this. George fucking Burns!

Adventures of a Subversive Cult Filmmaker from the Golden Age.

The door opened and an African American gentlemanly man appeared with a pleasant smile. I can't remember the man's name so I'll call him Jake. He was very polite and smartly dressed. Didn't seem like he did much heavy lifting around the Burns residence so I surmised that he was sort of a companion and aide to an elderly man living alone.

With Jake leading the way, Ms. Beard and I stepped into the house and off in the distance was this little guy seated on a long sofa in front of a bay window, puffing a cigar. Without getting up, he waved us over. Fuck me! Katy did the intros, presenting me and Ms. Beard as a couple as planned. We all joined George on the couch with the girls seated between me and George, which suited him just fine. George pretty much ignored me and after a little banter with the girls, an awkward silence blanketed the room. I started getting paranoid that this was going to be a very long, uncomfortable night. Just quietly puffing on his cigar, George was probably wondering what the hell he was thinking agreeing to this. A double date on a Saturday night with a couple of total strangers young enough to be his grandchildren, when he could've had his young sweetie all alone?

The sound of the doorbell broke the awkward silence. It was a group from the advertising agency who were in town for a *Sgt. Pepper* promotional photo shoot with George the following Monday. They were all on their way to dinner, but just wanted to introduce themselves and their wives to George. "Say hello to God!" was the clever intro they used. George was very gracious and puffed away at his cigar while they rattled on about how they used to listen to him and Gracie on the radio. After one of them asked the inevitable question about how he made the transition from vaudeville to radio, George looked down reflectively at the hand woven rug beneath his feet, took an even more reflective puff of his cigar, then, as if he hadn't answered that exact question twelve thousand times before said, "I asked Gracie how her brother was doing and she talked for the next twenty years."

He sat there, puffing his cigar, waiting for the follow up question. But it was too small a crowd and nobody was asking so I jumped in.

"So, how'd you go from radio to television?"

George shot a quick appreciative glance over to me, then said,

"Simple. I asked Gracie how her sister was doing and she talked for the next 10 years."

Everyone cracked up. But not George. It's way better to remain deadpan and pretend that he merely stated a fact and had no idea why they were laughing. George depended on a straight man, a set up man for most of his schtick, just the way he was the straight man for Gracie, so if I was to get the full comedic genius effect, I needed to play the role of his straight man for the night.

George and Jake walked the ad people to the door, then George came back and approached me.

"What ya drinkin' kid?"

"Kid…" That was ME he was referring to!

"I'll have anything you're drinking."

And of course the girls both said 'me too' and before you knew it, Jake mixed and served up a tray of four glistening vodka martinis, straight up to the brim.

"*L'Chaim*!" said George and we all took a slurp.

Now that George knew he had a straight man for the evening, his whole demeanor changed completely. He suddenly came alive, telling us stories, dropping names like a flash hailstorm: Jack Haley, Jack Benny, Jack Carter, Jackie Gleason… and those were just the Jacks!

Meanwhile, the martini was starting to hit me. Though the sixties were long over, I was still not a drinker and definitely NOT a straight martini drinker. Neither were the girls. George on the other hand seemed like he hadn't even had a drink. Or five.

When we set out for dinner, George led the way to the garage and his giant Cadillac, then he headed around for the driver's seat. No way I was letting him drive. Along with the alcohol it was doubtful he could really see over the steering wheel in that thing.

And he was 81. I insisted I drive. Not in his Caddy, in my rented Chevy.

So there we were, all sitting in my car in front of his house, me behind the wheel, George riding shotgun and the babes in the back seat, really getting giddy now from the sudden infusion of alcohol on their empty stomachs. It was beginning to actually feel like a date! And in fact, I was sensing that Ms. Beard wouldn't mind if I did pull a little funny business later on, even though that was clearly not part of the arrangement. I turned the key and the radio went on along with the engine, tuned to the rock station I had it set to when we pulled up. With the girls in the back seat and the music blasting it was like a scene out of "Hot Rods to Hell" with George sitting there, pleasantly puffing his cigar, feet barely touching the floor.

"So where we headed, kid?"

Crap. I hadn't made any dinner reservations. I thought Katy had. But it was no problem, George just asked everyone what they liked, and when we answered we liked pretty much everything he said, "How 'bout Le Dome?"

"Le Dome? Sure. But we need a reservation."

"So make one," George replied. "Tell 'em we'll be there in five minutes."

I cracked up. That was George's way of saying we didn't need one.

I drove up to the curb in front of Le Dome, the high end trendy Hollywood restaurant on Sunset Boulevard, the valet took the rental car and we all entered the front door with George leading the way. The maître d' lit up when he saw George, surveyed the size of our group then said, "Right this way Mister Burns!"

As we made our way to the special table they kept empty for just these occasions, everyone we passed stopped eating and either applauded, or made some reference to George being God while they reached out to shake his hand. And we were part of God's posse! The old trooper was very gracious to each and every one of them, while also acknowledging Hollywood types across the room with a wave of his cigar. Boy, how would George have functioned today when waving a lit cigar in the middle of a posh restaurant could get you arrested?

We all took our seats at the VIP table and the maître-d' handed us our menus. When George lifted his up to read it, the big menu completely obscured any view of him aside from the smoke billowing up. When the waiter arrived, George set his menu down.

"You kids order, I'm not ready. Have anything you want."

So George was picking up the tab for this? I assumed this was coming out of the *Sgt. Pepper* advertising budget but George considered this his private time and he was just out on a double date and being a sport. So we proceeded to order our entrees and main dishes while George studiously studied his menu. Finally, with our orders completed, the waiter circled around George who continued to study his menu.

"Have you decided, Mr. Burns?"

George flipped back a page for a quick review of the offerings, then finally folded his menu and set it down.

"How's the soup? Is the soup hot?"

"Oh, very hot, Mister Burns."

"Good. I'll have the soup."

That was it. That's all he ordered. And of course he knew that's what he'd be ordering before he even walked in the door. But waving off a menu and just telling a waiter all he wanted was a bowl of soup would not be funny. Reading over the entire menu from cover to cover, going back and re-examining it, then making the decision to just have soup as long as it's hot, IS funny. Classic Burns. And of course, along with being funny, this little bit, like most of George's material, was steeped in history. I had learned from my father that while growing up piss poor on New York's lower east side, hot soup was a luxury. What kind of soup was secondary, the most important thing on a cold wintery day was that it was hot.

George proceeded to do twenty minutes just on soup, and all the while delivering it as if he never said it before, which was his comic gift. And I was always right there with the right Gracie Allenesque setup questions he needed to keep things going. I have to mention that the waiter brought over four martinis without anyone ordering them. It was apparent that George was a regular at La Dome and they not only knew what he drank and how he liked it, straight up with one little onion, but since most dinner guests do the "I'll have what he's having" routine, they just took it upon themselves to make it martinis all around. At this point we've each had two filled to the brim gin martinis, and that's assuming George had waited for our arrival to enjoy his first cocktail of the evening, which was very unlikely. But then again, George wasn't counting.

As we headed back to George's house on Maple drive, there was no thought on any of our parts that I shouldn't be driving with three stiff drinks under my belt. I thought since I'd just be dropping him and Katy off at his house, then delivering Ms. Beard back to her place, it wouldn't be much driving back to my hotel. I pulled up to the curb on Maple drive and put my hand out to shake with George. But he just held on and said, "Come in for a night cap."

The idea of an after party with an 81 year old never occurred to me. I shut the engine, circled around the car and put out my arm to escort George to the door. By this time the girls were feeling no pain and when we entered the front door they immediately ordered more drinks from Jake. We all returned to the same long couch at the back of the living room. Now George was really letting his hair, or toupee down as he broke into a repertoire of limerick style songs, all memorized from his days in Vaudeville. Only he sang every word in Yiddish and no matter how much we begged him, he refused to translate. When the girls started doing a drunken minuet to his singing, I scooped up my drink and wandered off deeper into the house.

I wound up in the den at the front side of the house, which was still in sight of the goings-on in the living room. My attention was drawn to the fireplace mantle lined with family pictures of George, Gracie and Ronnie through the years. Then something else caught my eye, something on the floor, covered with dust. At first it appeared to be an old sports trophy that Ronnie might've won as a schoolboy. But when I looked closer it became clear it was an Academy Award! I pick it up, rubbed the dust off with my sleeve and read the inscription, 'Best supporting actor, George Burns, *The Sunshine Boys*.

I shouted to the back room, "Hey George! What's this Oscar doing on the floor? It should be up here on the mantle!"

With a wave of his cigar he called back to me, "Put that down kid, it don't belong to me, it belongs to Benny!" That rang a bell. I remembered reading about how that role was originally offered to Jack Benny, but when he became gravely ill he asked the producers and the director, Carl Reiner, to cast his best friend George Burns.

Under the exact same circumstances, most Hollywood types would not only have this Oscar sitting proudly on their mantle, but they'd have a special spotlight installed to draw attention to it. The fact the role was intended for their closest friend, not them, would never be mentioned. Regardless of the fact that it was George's performance that earned him the award, George actually felt it wasn't his. I got goose bumps. I was in the presence of the real deal. The rare kind of person my father taught me to always look out for. A *mensch* of the highest order.

So another round of drinks and it was now three in the morning and it was us youngsters, not George, who were ready to throw in the towel. On the way out the door I passed two boxes of cigars placed on a shelf for guests. I picked up a Dunhill Montecruz, which was a pretty expensive cigar. George said, "Take a handful kid."

I looked at him. "George, I can get these anywhere. I want one of yours."

"Mine? El Producto Queens? I've been smoking them for 60 years. They burn like a clothes line so I wouldn't so I have to keep re-lighting them during my act." They also cost around 30 cents apiece and they were probably made with a hefty helping of shirt cardboard mixed in with the tobacco.

George raised his hand to Jake and outstretched his hand, and an instant later a genuine El Producto Queen in a glass tube was handed to me. I held it in my hand, savoring the moment.

"George, you'll probably outlive me by a mile. But if by some freak chance you don't and I read that you're dead. You know, in *Variety*, like in *The Sunshine Boys*, that's when I'm gonna light this up."

Jeff Lieberman • Day Of The Living Me!

Right on the beat, George signaled again to Jake, this time with a writing motion and their special code produced a pen and paper. George scribbled something down, took the El Producto from my hand, removed it from the tube, and wrapped the note around the cigar. Then he tucked it back into my pocket and patted it. Instead of shaking his hand goodbye, for some reason I felt compelled to kiss him on the forehead, then Jake showed me and Ms. Beard out the door.

As we approached the car, Ms. Beard asked the obvious question, "Aren't you gonna read it?"

I took it out and under the landscape lighting I could read it without removing the cigar from the tube. It read, "To Jeff, don't smoke it." And signed George Burns. I laughed because it was his response to what I said about him dying and that if I was smoking it, it meant he just died. However...

CUT TO: Nineteen years later, George celebrated his 100th birthday and I still had that cigar proudly displayed in my office, with a special light shining on it as if it was my own Oscar. The years had not been kind to that El Producto Queen, and in fact, it looked more like something excavated from Tutankhamun's tomb. It was sort of mummified, shriveled up under George's rapidly yellowing note, but still encased in its original glass tube.

Not long after George's milestone birthday I heard it on the news. Not from *Variety*, but every news agency in the multi-platform, Internet saturated, instant news delivery system of the day. George Burns, dead at age 100. He didn't outlive me after all. I shook up a martini, raised my glass and said a final *l'chaim* to the man. Then I remembered what I told him that night during our final moments together, that I'd smoke that cigar when I got that news of his passing. Now I had to keep my promise.

Scores of my friends called me the instant they heard the news because they had all seen the cigar and the note it was encased in and heard the story behind it. What should I do? In situations like this, moralistic decisions that reach Talmudic proportions, I will always defer to my older brother. This was his advice:

"So, he wrote, "To Jeff, don't smoke it?" Maybe he knew that by the time he actually died, that cigar which was marginally smokable to begin with, would more resemble a piece of petrified wood, so if you did smoke it then YOU'D die and he was trying to warn you."

Even though that was clearly bullshit, my brother knew I didn't want to smoke it because I cherished the memory of George with this little memento.

106

Adventures of a Subversive Cult Filmmaker from the Golden Age.

It gave me an out that George himself would appreciate.

So I didn't smoke it. And to this day, that tube containing that mummified El Producto Queen sits proudly on my office shelf, right beside the dust-covered Emmy award I would win later on down the line.

George Burns' El Producto

16. BLUE SUNSHINE

Shooting an independent movie on locations in Los Angles in the late 1970's presented a challenge I never thought about until I came face to face with it. Every television movie at that time was shot on similar budgets and used so many of the same locations I'd be using, how could I avoid my movie to lookinig like an episode of Starsky and Hutch or just another TV movie of the week? I finally realized the answer was in the material, not the budget or locations. LSD was not a subject you'd find in any network Movie of the Week. I also tried to employ cinematic camera moves and compositions that would never be used in a straightforward television movie. In short, I was going for a certain look, but that required extra time that I didn't have which in turn put that much more pressure on me.

The premise of the movie was scientifically far-fetched so I didn't want to take any more factual liberties than I already had in the script. This became a challange when we shot a key suspenseful scene at a real hospital operating room and nobody on the production had a clue as to what a real operation looked like. Sure, talented actor Robert Walden playing a surgeon looked the part in his operating scrubs, as did the actresses playing his nurses, but what were all those sadistic looking operating tools called, and more importantly, what where they used for? On a larger budget we'd have a medical advisor standing by for accuracy but in this case the only advisor I could think of was my brother Gary.

Since we could only gain access to the operating room at night, I had no choice but to wake him up at two in the morning east coast time, knowing full well he'd assume someone died.

After being assured that nobody died, he explained that since he'd chosen to pursue pediatrics, his only exposure to general surgery was in medical school and he could only remember the name of two instruments.

"One's called a "long instrument."

"Great! What's it look like?"

"It's long."

"How long?"

"I don't know, pick the longest one."

"Okay, what's the other one?"

"A Kelly."

"What's that look like?"

"Like a long scissor."

"How long?"

"I don't know, they're all sizes, they're all called Kellys."

So that was the extent of our on-set medical consultations. If you watch that scene, Robert Walden calls for a Kelly and a long instrument ten times more than an actual surgeon ever would because those are the only names we knew. Of course my brother earned the title of Medical Advisor in the closing credits as compensation for waking him up in the middle of the night.

LSD-crazed babysitter, *Blue Sunshine* 1977

Blue Sunshine cast: L to R top row Marc Goddard, me. Second row: Zalman King, Deborah Winters and Robert Walden. Bottom: Jeffry Druce

109

17. LOW ON OIL WITH SIDNEY POITIER

Though my career was focused on making independent genre movies, I still maintained a relationship with the top brass at Janus, Saul Turell and Bill Becker, and after *Blue Sunshine* was behind me in 1979 I reunited to co-produce and direct a documentary called *Museum* financed by the Arthur Sackler Foundation for PBS. I didn't want to be pigeonholed as a *horror-meister* so a highbrow project like this came along at the perfect time.

While I was shooting *Museum* for Janus Productions, Saul was working on his own personal passion project, a documentary on the great singer-actor Paul Robeson who was blackballed by Hollywood for his communist party affiliations. Saul was a throwback from the time a thoughtful person could express what seemed to be contradictory views but if when assessed objectively wouldn't seem contradictory or hypocritical at all. He was a very big supporter of Richard Nixon, actually wrote him letters of advice during the Watergate scandal. He compared him to Tom Swift and was convinced that Nixon wouldn't lie. But he always made it clear he was on the side of the civil rights struggle and Robeson's story needed to be told. Saul wrote the narration along with Paul Robeson Jr. who also helped him gain access to rare archival material.

I was completely consumed with filming *Museum* and had nothing at all to do with Saul's pet project. One day while I was laying plans to film the arrival of the first appearance of the Tutankhamun exhibition in the states which was to be assembled in the Met's Sackler wing around set against the Temple of Dendur, Saul shared that he decided he'd have Paul Robeson Jr. narrate his documentary. Seeing the positive results I got from Rod Serling, he asked if I'd like to sit in on the session. As much as I wanted to butt out of

Adventures of a Subversive Cult Filmmaker from the Golden Age.

Saul's passion project, I couldn't help butting in instead.

"You want Paul Jr. to narrate it?"

"Sure, why not?"

"Saul, 16 people know who Paul Robeson was and only two of them are black. If you want this thing to get any attention, you need to get the most famous black personality on the planet to narrate it."

"That's pie in the sky."

"No it's not. Paul Robeson? No famous black guy would turn that down. Or could turn it down. Lots of good publicity for furthering the civil rights cause, and it'll probably win a freaking Oscar. Or at least get nominated. Saul, it's the kind of documentary that nobody in Hollywood actually watches, but they'll all pretend they did and vote for it to show each other, and their kids, how liberal and committed to the cause they are."

I was merely applying what I learned from my father about how things work. Not how people would like them to work but how they actually do. The way he raised money for various charities relying on powerful personalities to bring in donations regardless of the cause applied directly to this.

"Got it. Sidney Poitier."

Saul laughed out loud.

"Sure. Terrific. Just call him up!"

"You want me to?"

"You know him?"

"No. But give me a half hour and I'll get him."

"You're on!"

There were only three major talent agencies at the time, William Morris, ICM and CMA, so it only took me five minutes to find out which one represented Sidney and another five to get the phone number of his manager. Naturally the manager wasn't going to take my call so I left a message with his assistant that specifically laid out who Paul Robeson was and how Sidney being an activist for civil rights would give gravitas to the film and in turn, garner attention to Robeson's heroic struggle. Not certain I laid it on as thick as "gravitas" but that was the gist. Then I threw in the prestige of Janus Films to make sure he knew Sidney would be in the hands of a respected, class operation, just as I did with Rod Serling.

Twenty minutes later the manager himself called back, wanting further details. I told him the film was cut and we'd fly Sidney to New York first class to do the recording, which would only require one afternoon in the studio. Twenty-five minutes after that the manager called back again saying Sidney agreed to do it but under the condition it's done in LA where he lived. I agreed.

I returned to Saul's office, slumped down in the chair and checked my watch. "Okay, I lied. It took me forty five minutes."

"You got him?"

"Yep. Only hitch is you have to record him in LA."

"Okay, no problem! Would you come?"

"Sure, why not?"

Though Saul wanted me to direct Sidney, he didn't want to use the word "direct" since he was the director of this film and I actually had no official role in it at all. That was fine with me, this was Saul's baby. I considered it doing a favor for a friend. Maybe even a little payback for all he'd done for me since I'd done some serious riding on his back as well.

One week later Saul and I were driving our rental car through the front gates of a stately Beverly Hills mansion located a couple of blocks behind the Beverly Hills Hotel. The place was teaming with groundskeepers.

A beautiful young blonde barefoot woman wearing a man's dress shirt in place of a nightgown greeted us at the front door. I later learned she was actress Joanna Shimkus who had recently given up her acting career to marry Sidney. Joanna was charming as can be, offered us some scrambled eggs which we declined, then showed us to the library, which was as big as a two-room apartment in New York.

The centerpiece of the room was a gigantic fireplace that seemed like a replica of the magnificent stone-carved piece in the movie *Citizen Kane*. Sidney emerged from a sunken leather couch to greet us, shook our hands, then gestured for us to take a seat while he remained standing.

I started to talk about where we'd be recording, asking for any notes Sidney had on the script, nuts and bolts stuff, but Sidney had other things on his mind. Pacing the room, with a serious concerned expression he started lecturing us about how third world countries, particularly in Africa, were now gaining access to videotape. The VCR format. "They gather in the village centers and watch the tapes, which to many of them is their first contact with the outside world. And what are they being given to watch?" He waited a beat for full dramatic effect.

"*I Love Lucy!*" Sidney's point was that they should be watching films on how to grow their own crops using modern methods, educational films in their own languages, things like that, and he wanted us to produce the videos.

Adventures of a Subversive Cult Filmmaker from the Golden Age.

Saul was so enamored with Sidney's presence I think he would've agreed to anything. "Great idea!" he said.

There was no possible way I was making farming films. I'd go back to doing Excedrin commercials before I'd do that. But I tried to muster some enthusiasm so as not to present any obstacles to getting this narration done.

"Good!" Now Sidney picked up a poker from the fireplace, then dramatically turned and pointed it at both of us. "Petrol! We're running out of petrol gentlemen!"

Since this was the era of the great oil embargo, the scarcity of oil was a front and center issue with all the Hollywood activists. And since Sidney was very issue-oriented, he thought it urgent to make educational films on that subject too. "Do you realize that third world countries are trying to emulate us? Our ways? Our lifestyle of consumption? Two cars in every driveway, four TVs in every house. In China, a country of over a billion people, they're forming a middle class and buying automobiles, and with it comes a massive demand for petrol. India, everywhere in the third world they're striving to own cars, run industries the way we do in the west, all dependent on an exploding consumption of petrol!"

What in hell was this? We didn't fly across the country to get lectured on the social issues of the day. And I was really getting annoyed that he kept saying "petrol" instead of "oil." Who the hell says "petrol" unless they're reading from an encyclopedia? The more he said it, the more it irritated me.

Another ten minutes of laying the groundwork and he set down the poker and stood there in front of the towering fireplace mantle and narrowed his eyes on us. All I could think of was "don't say petrol anymore, please don't say petrol..." But he did. Twice. "Do you realize that if all those poor countries catch up to us, live like us and consume the same amount of petrol as we do in this country, the world will run out of petrol in ten years?"

The New Yorker in me couldn't take any more of this and it just came out, "If everyone in *this* country lived like you do, we'd run out of petrol in two weeks!"

Sidney's eyes widened with surprise, while Saul's face drained to a chalky white. Did I just blow the whole deal? The moment was very reminiscent of the time I told Joe Carlo and Matty the Horse that Jews don't beat their wives, Italians do. I just can't help it. Many have accused me of not having a filter over the years, but I swear it's an involuntary reaction to bullshit. And magically, Sidney reacted the same way those wise guys did with a loud hearty laugh and a big slap me five gesture. "C'mon, let's do this!" he said, and we were off to the recording studio without another mention of petrol.

On the way to the studio Sidney told us how great it was to be with real New Yorkers, which I took to mean people who treated him like a regular person and called him on his bullshit when warranted. There's not a lot of that when you're one of the top movie stars in the world and surrounded by agents, managers and an adoring public every day.

He told us he was from a very poor family in the Bahamas, which back then were under British rule. I thought to myself, "Well, that explains why he says 'petrol' instead of 'oil.'" I felt like a complete schmuck, but my repeating his use of the word the way I did didn't seem to bother him at all as he continued to reminisce about New York. Then he gazed down and formed a sweet smile.

"Know what I miss most? Leaves in the fall."

The recording went great. Saul's narration copy was smooth and easy for Sidney to make it his own. Probably the easiest direction I ever gave an actor. But hell, he was Sidney fucking Poitier!

That fall, I grabbed a FedEx box from the office and brought it to Central park where I filled it with an assortment of colored leaves. Then I sent it off to Sidney with the inscription, "To Sir, with love." - Jeff

The following March, Saul J. Turell won the Academy Award for best documentary short, *Paul Robeson, Portrait of an Artist*, narrated by Sidney Poitier.

18. THE TUT CURSE

After that short detour I picked up where I left off on the *Museum* documentary just in time for shooting the Tutankhamun exhibition's arrival at the Met. Because the film was being financed by Arthur Sackler who was also a major benefactor of the museum, we were given exclusive access to shoot the arrival, uncrating, and setting up of those priceless artifacts. Phillipe de Montebello, the director of the Met, made it clear to me he was the go-to man if any problems arose. We got along really well and in no time I was calling him 'Phil,' just like I did with Philippe Petite. He didn't seem to mind at all and in fact shared some incredible museum secrets which he made me swear to keep secret so you ain't gonna hear it here.

Unfortunately our special treatment didn't extend to letting us know exactly when the Tut exhibition would arrive. All the advanced publicity of these historic artifacts going on a US tour for the first time created a security nightmare. The Egyptian government wouldn't allow the press any information on even when the stuff would arrive at Kennedy airport let alone the museum, so I had to keep a film crew on call twenty four-seven.

Fortunately, that expensive arrangement only lasted two days until I finally got a late afternoon heads-up from the museum and I scrambled to round up the crew and equipment to shoot the late night arrival of a convoy of unmarked trucks. We set up in the dark expansive basement level freight area of the Met just in time to shoot the trucks rolling down the ramp.

Armed guards stood by while several wooden crates were loaded onto the dock. I made sure to film the entire scene, with Phil and a group of his Egyptian curators standing alongside a team of very serious and official-looking Egyptian government types while experts wearing surgical gloves to avoid any contamination carefully lifted each piece from its crate. Then a hush blanketed the entire proceeding, which heightened the dramatic effect of this historic occasion. After thousands of years the Boy King had finally made it to the Big Apple.

Phil's people were looking for any signs of damage that might have occurred during the trip overseas before signing off and turning over responsibility to the Met's insurance liability for the run of the exhibition. So this was very serious stuff and I had a front row seat. And so did our camera!

The most impressive and dramatic moment came when one of the crates revealed a complex, two-section, alabaster piece held together with what would later be commercialized as "Tut glue." It was very delicate and required four of the surgical-gloved men to keep it steady so the ancient glue seam wouldn't crack. Everyone held their collective breath as they balanced it in the air trying not to tilt it then finally set it down. A relieved Phil broke decorum and applauded excitedly, then the others followed suit.

"That's gonna make one hell of a shot," I thought. I couldn't wait to see the dailies. But then my cameraman slipped in close to me and whispered something that made my blood run cold. He confided that he wasn't rolling and didn't get any of it!

"What? Oh shit!" This wasn't a dramatic movie where that sort of bad news was common, and everyone would just react with moans and groans while they re-set for another take. With documentaries there were no take-twos. But my filmmaking instincts said the hell with the rules; I can't bear not having this in the movie. But how in hell am I gonna make that happen? Ask them to just put it back in the crate and lift it out again when I call "action?" They'd have to be out of their minds to do that. What if it broke apart on the second try? The Egyptians would be up the Nile without a paddle. And the Met would be on the hook too for permitting me to film it.

But fuck, I had to have it so I dashed over to Phil and took him aside. Anyone else would've said "Are you fucking crazy? Take your people and the cameras and get the hell out of here!" But Phil was way too genteel for that. He genuinely sympathized with my situation and also wanted to show off his museum in the best possible light. I held my breath as he went over to the Egyptians and explained the situation as faces all registered astonishment, then they all looked over to me, exchanged incredulous looks with each other, then lifted the piece and set it back in the crate.

My cameraman reset his position and I took over. "Okay, sure you're rolling now?"

Adventures of a Subversive Cult Filmmaker from the Golden Age.

He nodded. "Okay, the uncrating of the alabaster, take two. Action!"

Once again the Tut glue came through and held those two priceless pieces together as they were lifted out and set down on a blanket.

Around two A.M. we broke for lunch and I found myself all alone in the vast darkened expanse of the Sackler wing. The Temple of Dendur was illuminated in the distance and I moseyed over to the glimmering iconic golden bust of the boy king encased in glass and mounted atop a pedestal near the entrance.

The designers of the exhibition knew the public was attracted to gold and that the bust would be the focal piece of the exhibition so they set it at a height that would calibrate the eyes to a five foot ten inch visitor, the average male tourist. Since that was very near to my own height (at the time) I couldn't resist stepping up close and looking the little bastard right in the eye. It was just me and Tut, mano y boyo. And I let him have it.

"Fuck you Tut! And every fucking Egyptian who ever whipped a Hebrew slave. And fuck Yul Brynner too!"

All he could do was silently stare back at me, too scared to move. No earth moving rumbling. No lightning. No mummies coming to life. Nothing. So much for the Tut curse.

Next day at Janus I was eagerly awaiting the report on the dailies from the Tut shoot. A fellow named Bob Schmitt who handled all things labs and shipping came into the conference room, looking a tad somber as he took a drag on a cigarette.

"Just got a call from the lab. Everything looks great except a problem on one roll. Deep irreparable negative camera scratch through the whole thing."

"Holy shit," I thought, "the curse! It's real!" It was a foregone conclusion which reel it was. Tut clearly heard me curse him out from the great beyond in his cushy, peeled grape eating afterlife and his answer was (loosely translated from the Egyptian) "Fuck me? No Hebrew, fuck you!"

I told Schmitt I knew which reel and shot it was. "The role of the close-up headshot of the Tut bust."

"How'd you know?"

"The curse."

19. THE FIRST FEMINIST HORROR MOVIE?

While finishing up on the *Museum* documentary I got a mysterious call from a man with a very heavy Czechoslovakian accent.

"Hello? Is this the Jeff Lieberman?"

"Yeah."

"You did the *Squirms*?"

"Uh, yeah. Who's this?"

"This is Doro Vlado Hreljanovic. So you'll come and maybe you'll do for us?"

"Do what?"

"We have the George Kennedy and the Linda Blair. So you'll come and you'll do? Come to our offices and discuss."

I hung up with no clue as to what that was all about until I received a follow-up call from someone I knew who had given this Vlado fellow my number. He explained that Vlado was a legitimate movie producer who had earned an academy award nomination for best foreign film for the Milos Foreman-directed *Loves of a Blonde*, which I was a big fan of back in film school. He was looking for a director so he was given my number at Janus. I agreed to meet Vlado at his offices located on the corner of Broadway and 57th street, a space he took over from none other than Robert Stigwood, which I took as a good omen.

The screenplay Vlado presented me was called *The Last Ritual*, changed from the original title *The Tennessee Mountain Murders*. Vlado explained that he was given a short list of directors who had approval from foreign financing and I was on that list. So along with George Kennedy and Linda Blaire, if I signed on, the movie would be a go. "Wow," I thought, an instant movie deal based on the fact that I 'did the *Squirms*.' Sounded too good to be true.

And when I got home and read the thing, reality slapped me in face. The script was an abomination. The story centered on some Hillbilly snake worshippers in the Smokey Mountains who terrorize a group of young campers, force one of them into marrying them, which requires idiotic scenes of religious snake handling rituals. Hence the title, *The Last Ritual*. The screenplay didn't even look professional with long-winded descriptions that sometimes filled entire pages, and it even included illustrations like some ill-conceived adult version of a children's book.

My first instinct was to just throw the thing in the trash bin and pass on the project like those other 'bankable' directors on Vlado's list must've done before me. That was my creative instinct. My artistic instinct. But then my mortgage with a family instinct took over along with the realization that I was the key to the financing at this point and that gave me leverage I never had before. It got me thinking, what if I could transform this into something creatively appealing to me?

I thought about it all night and the next day it came to me. John Boorman's movie *Deliverance* had a tremendous impact on me, as did the book it was based on. It harkened back to *Lord of the Flies*, another big influencer in formulating my views of seeing humans as little more than hairless apes. Removed from modern society and put in a position of survive or die, humans will revert to their primal selves. The beasts within us.

This idea was illustrated by John Voight's mild-mannered milquetoast character joining a group of friends venturing downriver in the Georgia wilds. Little by little Voight evolved, or devolved, tapping into his primitive instincts to survive. What if I assigned that same character arch to a woman, one of this group of young campers in the screenplay?

When I pitched this all to Vlado he seemed receptive but also cautioned me not to change it too much, that it'd scare the buyers who already signed off on it. One of the key things I promised was to keep the main group of character's names so if a buyer were to flip through the re-worked script it would appear to be what they bought. Vlado's people introduced me to the writer of the original script with the idea that we'd work on the rewrite together. He was a nice enough fellow but I saw no point in this at all. Anyone who'd write a script like that wouldn't be of any help to me so I insisted on doing it alone. Being the original writer, he'd still get co-writing credit even if I rewrote it from page one. Which is exactly what I wound up doing.

First piece of business was to go through the script with a black marker and X out all scenes and references to snakes, the rituals and the religious stuff that went with it. All of it. So one thing was certain, it wasn't going to be called The *Last Ritual* anymore.

I renamed it *Just Before Dawn* based on a notion that the climactic scene where the character of Connie completes her transition to her animal survivor state would occur at that magical time right before first daylight.

I assumed Connie would be played by Linda Blair until I learned she was just a name used to raise money. I never got a straight answer as to whether she ever even knew about the project. But George Kennedy was real and on board pending the re-write, so I custom-fitted his character of Roy the forest ranger with some likable eccentricities, like talking to his horse Agatha. And his house plants. When George read the finished script, he signed right on.

Instead of the Smoky Mountains we decided to shoot the movie out west, either northern California or Oregon and set up our production offices in Los Angeles. Since I had very few contacts with production people out there and needed to put together a good non-union crew I could depend on, I took the easy route and called John Carpenter. John worked with many of the same people on each movie and I fortunately caught them between projects so it was instant crew - just add contracts.

Next piece of business was to nail down our locations, which required mountainous wilderness. A trip to the Redwood Forest convinced me that we had to go further north to achieve that isolated feeling I was looking for. We booked flights from LAX to Salem, Oregon, figuring we'd rent a car there and head on into the national forests at the foot of the Cascade Mountains.

When we arrived at LAX there was a big crowd around our gate area. Then we looked up at the board, which said our flight was cancelled. Why? A volcanic eruption! Mount Saint Helens, located about fifty miles northeast of Portland, had unleashed its fury, seriously screwing up our schedule.

It wasn't until five days later that flights to Salem resumed. The city was covered with volcanic ash which looked a lot like snow. Turned out the Silver Lake National Forest suited the script perfectly so we were all set.

Our cast members wound up being Greg Henry whom I'd seen on *Rich Man, Poor Man*, and Deborah Benson, Ralph Seymour and Jamie Rose, all of whom I cast based on their impressive auditions. Chris Lemmon got the nod also based on his audition but it never hurts on a low budget movie to have some "name value" for publicity purposes, and the son of Jack Lemmon scored points in that area. I actually met Jack at a restaurant around that time because someone told him I would be directing Chris. Jack came over to my table, leaned into my ear and said, "Don't take any of his shit." It was clear to me they had a good relationship as I would later develop with Chris myself during the shoot and over the years.

Then there was George Kennedy. *Cool Hand Luke*! I'd actually be directing an academy award winner!

When the time came to shoot George's scenes I was told that his contract stipulated that although he's adept at riding a horse, he couldn't be filmed either mounting nor dismounting. They didn't offer any reason and it was a non-negotiable requirement in any contract he signed that required horseback riding. I told my assistant director, Fred Berner, about the strange stipulation in George's contract, and that I wanted to be tipped off when George was about to get on his horse for his scenes.

When the night came for George to ride up to the hillbilly Logan family cabin, Fred gave me the heads up that George was about to mount up about thirty yards from where we were shooting. Once out of the radius of our movie lights it was pitch black but we saw a work light between the trees and made our way there just as two Teamsters, one for each leg, were lifting George onto the saddle stomach down. The horse started to rotate in circles with George sprawled across the saddle and the two men following trying to get one of his legs over the other side to straddle the horse. When they finally did, George was able to sit up, slide his boots into the stirrups and then take the reins. The transition was amazing, going from someone who seemed he'd never been on a horse in his life to an actor who's ridden in a million cowboy movies. Which he had. He just couldn't mount or dismount. Hey, neither can I.

In 2017 I appeared with *Just Before Dawn* at the Alamo Drafthouse in Denver and Walter Chaw the programmer at that time introduced the movie as "the first feminist horror movie." I was a little taken aback at the sound of that, but I guess it is. The character of Connie turned out to be considered one of the earlier modern archetypes of what would later be termed the "final girl," the leading lady in horror movies that was either the last to die, or be saved by a male hero. In *Just Before Dawn* though, the final girl saves herself and her boyfriend in a gender role reversal and act of primal violence equal to anything a man can do.

Jeff Lieberman • Day Of The Living Me!

Over the years the movie has grown in stature with both fans and academics and is now being grouped along with *The Texas Chainsaw Massacre*, *Halloween*, *The Hills Have Eyes* and *Friday the 13th* as part of the so-called "Golden Age of Horror" and its sub-genre of 'slasher' movies. Who knew?

Left to right, A.D. Fred Berner, Jeff, Greg Henry and Deborah Benson

Deborah Benson, Jeff and Greg Henry

Adventures of a Subversive Cult Filmmaker from the Golden Age.

A moment of meditation with George Kennedy before the camera rolls.

Deborah Benson traversing rope bridge

20. GOING HOLLYWOOD

Around that time in the early and mid-eighties the subject of artificial insemination was making front-page headlines on newspapers and magazines like Life and Time. New technologies always spawn new federal guidelines, which concentrate on risks and dangers rather than their benefits to society. A whole list of 'what if's' was posited by the so-called experts on fertility and genetics. What if we start creating designer babies, look for high IQ donors to create little Einsteins, or super athletes, or the identities of the donors are later revealed to children in search of their biological fathers?

Since 'what if's' triggered so many of my ideas over the years, especially when spawned by a new scientific breakthrough with deep sociological implications, I immediately came up with a what if of my own; what if a donor sperm was given to the wrong recipient? Bingo, I knew right away this held the potential for a movie. At this point I had actually learned how to type and immediately pounded out the words, 'Mating Calls' on my new IBM selectric.

We had decided to make the move to Los Angeles but were not ready to sell the house that Squirm built so we rented it out for two years to an executive at CBS. I finished writing the Mating Calls screenplay and sent it out to my new Los Angeles agent, Marion Rosenberg, who liked it and submitted it to a producer named Jennings Lang who also responded positively enough to set up a meeting with me as soon as I got settled in LA. Marion presented me as the director of the movie as well.

In the interim, I did some research on Jennings and it was immediately clear that this guy was big time, real old school Hollywood. One of the last of the authentic movie moguls. At Universal, Jennings had produced and executive-produced movies like *Play Misty for Me*, *Charley Varrick*,

Adventures of a Subversive Cult Filmmaker from the Golden Age.

Slaughterhouse Five, Airport, Earthquake, and most recently *The Sting Two.* But more impressive to me was that he'd been head of Universal Television in the late 50's and 60's overseeing many of the shows I grew up on like *Wagon Train, The Bob Cummings Show* and *McHale's Navy.*

A few weeks later we were settled in a rental house in West Los Angeles and the meeting was set at Jenning's office on the Universal studio lot in Burbank. After his stint as VP of production ended, Jennings moved from the famed 'black tower' executive building to legendary costume designer Edith Head's old bungalow, which was located among the sound stages and right along the route of the popular Universal studio tour.

I pulled into one of the two visitors spaces next to a beautiful classic Mercedes convertible. Towering above me were two huge 'coming soon' movie billboards, one for Steven Speilberg's movie *E.T.* and the other for *The Sting Two,* starring Jackie Gleason and Mack Davis. And just under the title the words 'produced by Jennings Lang.' Holy shit, this is the big time Hollywood I thought as I turned and entered the bungalow.

Inside, Jennings secretary Jane greeted me warmly and asked me to take a seat in the outer office waiting room while Jennings finished up with a closed-door meeting.

"Feels like I'm in a dentist's office," I quipped.

"Actually, a lot of people leave here in worse pain than that after Jennings gets finished with them," she counter-quipped.

I got the sense that she was only half kidding and suddenly started losing my cool, which was crucial to me in this kind of circumstance. About ten minutes later the door opened and out walked Michael 'O Donoghue, 'Mr. Mike,' head writer of and performer of the original *Saturday Night Live* and also of *National Lampoon* fame. Given that he was an infamously strange manic-depressive to begin with, he didn't look any worse for wear from weathering a meeting with Jennings. Jane's buzzer rang.

"Okay Jeff, you can go in now."

I entered and Jennings rose from his chair with a big grin. A big man, at least three inches taller than me, he graciously offered me a drink from his fully stocked bar. A drink? Usually at these meetings you're offered ten varieties of designer water or six varieties of coffee. But Jennings was old school all the way and was obviously not a designer water kind of guy. I declined and took a seat in front of his desk. After chatting about my script he said he held off on optioning it because he doesn't like to just tie up properties. If he options anything he intends to follow through and make the movie, so he wanted to know how amenable I was to input and notes because he had a lot of ideas to incorporate into further re-writes. After assuring him that I was always open to making something better, especially when it'd still have my name on it as 'written by,' which he laughed at, he leaned forward, folded his hands on his desk and looked me dead in the eye.

"Your agent sent me your movie, *Just Before Dawn*? I watched half of it, okay I guess, not my kind of thing those B-movies.'

So much for my directing this I thought.

"So you worked with George Kennedy. How'd you get along?"

"Fine. I guess."

"He think you're any good? As a director?"

"Dunno. I think so."

He punched a button on his phone.

"Jane, get me George Kennedy."

What? I couldn't believe this guy. Calling George Kennedy at home and right off the bat he asks what he thought of Jeff Lieberman as a director. No mention at all that I was sitting right in front of him and could hear every word on speaker.

It was brutal. Jane was right, this was worse than root canal. Clearly Jennings wanted a true assessment of me as a director from an academy award-winning actor and if there was anything negative, he wanted for me to hear it too so I'd know exactly why he was passing. This guy really played hardball and all I wanted to do was duck.

Fortunately, George thought very highly of me, used the word 'super' over and over. Then the two of them made a dinner date with 'the wives,' Jennings hung up and that was it. He'd be calling my agent to option my screenplay, along with a deal for a re-write and if the picture gets made, it'll be with me directing.

So just like that our trip out to LA already paid off. The money I'd make from that one deal alone, just the option and re-writes was good for a whole year of our expenses, moving included. Hollywood!

My estranged mentor, Ernie Pintoff, with whom I had no contact for a good ten years, had also re-located to Los Angeles and was directing for television. I really missed Ernie and thought it was worth a shot to see if his grudge had dissipated over time so I got his number and called him.

Ernie sounded genuinely happy to hear from me and we yacked for at least a half hour catching up on the years we missed together which included Ernie directing episodes of Kojack which stemmed from his experience on Blade. When we got to the present, Ernie asked what I'm working on now and when I mentioned the name Jennings Lang he corrected me.

"Jenning."

"Ernie, your wrong, his name's Jennings. I'm tellin' ya. I was just with the guy."

"Jeff. JennING. He used to be Jennings until he got shot in the nuts by a jealous husband who caught him schtupping his wife, some actress. From then on he was Jenning, only one ball."

Turned out Ernie was right about Jennings having an affair with married actress Joan Bennett and was caught in the act by her husband Producer Walter Wanger who shot Jennings in the groin. Rumors quickly spread through Hollywood circles that one of Jennings jewels were blasted off and from that spawned the nickname Jenning which was used behind his back ever since. Well, from my first impression of Jennings, even if the story was true he was doing quite well with just one and I needed both to stay in this game that was officially morphing into a career.

One day, riding in Jenning's Mercedes convertible on our way to Chasins, one of the go-to restaurants of the Hollywood crowd, Jennings turned to me matter-of-factly.

"Your agent called asking for a ten grand payment you're due on this last pass. If you need it now, when we get back to the lot I'll cut you a check then I'll get re-imbursed from the studio."

I looked at him incredulously.

"Jennings. You think I'd move my family out here to deal with people like you and need ten grand to eat?"

A slow smile formed on his face along with a little nod of recognition. That was the exact moment we bonded.

From then on Jennings took me into his inner circle, all centered around his Beverly Hills nine-bedroom mansion at 606 Mountain Drive. My first time there he took me on a tour. The house had a professional regulation tennis court complete with judges stand, a huge pool and a pool house that contained none other than an actual pool table used in the classic movie *The Hustler*. I just had to grab a pool cue and shoot a break shot. But before I did, I also felt obliged to recount the closing lines between Fast Eddie Felson and Minnesota Fats.

"Fat man, you shoot a great game of pool."

Jennings came right back with,

"So do you, Fast Eddie."

Bam! I made the break. What a fucking thrill that was!

Jennings put JoAnn and I on his regular Saturday night guest list for premiere screenings at the house. He had a union projectionist who worked for the studio come to the house every weekend to screen the latest movies in distribution. Our fellow regulars included great people like actor Darin McGavin and *Mission Impossible* composer Lilo Shifran. Clint Eastwood was a regular too but unfortunately we never turned up at the same time he did. Everyone arrived about an hour before the screenings and immediately the booze started flowing. By the time the movies rolled it was more like a loud drunken cocktail party than a screening, with the occasional loud 'shhh!' coming from anyone who was actually paying attention.

Because Jennings had actually brought Sid Sheinberg into the studio when he was a young lawyer, Jennings had direct access to him on his projects, side stepping the head of production as if he were a mailroom worker. When Jennings optioned my script he arranged to introduce me to Sid at his office at the Universal black tower. Talk about intimidating, this was the office where all of Steven Spielberg's movies were green lit, along with dozens of other blockbusters. Since my script was a comedy, Sid shared a formula he and Jennings concocted over a long trial and error process. It's all about blocks. Blocks of comedy. He explained that a block is measured from the time the audience starts laughing to the time it stops. It could be only one scene but more often it's a sequence that could even contain a hilarious car chase. He used the food fight scene from *Animal House* as one example since it was one of his movies. The true measure of a block is that audiences will likely recount it to other people creating positive word of mouth. How many times have you heard someone say "You gotta see this movie. It's got this one scene where..."

And that one scene could sell a potential ticket buyer to plunk down his money. So with one solid block you'll recoup your money. With two blocks you have a hit movie. And three blocks you have a blockbuster. What happens between blocks has only one function, to get the audience to the next block. Nobody will talk about or even remember the expositional scenes that made for the coherent narrative that allowed those blocks to happen.

So basically, this was the formula they came up with and their measure of every entertainment they made. 'Entertainment.' That was another term these moguls used. They separated serious social message movies like *Shindler's List* from entertainments like *Fast Times at Ridgemont High*. I of course was doing an entertainment, which I took as 'don't take this too seriously kid.'

Our meeting was periodically interrupted by the head of distribution excitedly barging in to give Sid the latest box office numbers. I felt like I was sitting inside Hollywood Central, seeing first hand what goes on behind the scenes in the real world of big time movie making. Intimidating? Nah. Shellshocked is a more accurate term. Here's another fine mess I'd gotten myself into!

Jennings would talk to me about everything and anything Hollywood, salacious stories about famous people both dead and living. Who did what to who, who stabbed who in the back, who fucked their way to the top, how certain people got their high position jobs in the most underhanded ways. The most fascinating stuff to me was how studios went into feeding frenzies over the next new thing, the next breakout new star. Roles that were written for white females were suddenly offered to overnight sensations like Eddie Murphy. 'We can change her to a man. We can make him black, no problem.' The experience was like listening to an audio version of the *National Enquirer, Hollywood Babylon,* and *People* magazine rolled into one, only Jennings knew all this dirt first hand. But he never brought up the subject of getting shot in the nuts by a jealous husband. Curious as I was to hear the story, I knew not to ask him about it because if he wanted me to know he would've brought it up himself.

We'd meet for lunch around twice a week to discuss the latest script changes and on those days I'd get a call from Jenning's assistant Jane asking which restaurant I'd prefer that day. Sometimes Jennings would jump on.

"How 'bout Spago. Feel like a little pasta?"

"Sure, whatever you want."

Later Jane explained to me that top studio people held special reserved tables at a handful of trendy restaurants of that time like Chasens, Scandia or The Ivy. Then by twelve noon they'd know where they decided to lunch that day and their assistants would call the other restaurants to alert them to release their usual tables in time to make them available to the public. Jennings took talent to these power lunches, actors, writers, directors, for them to see and be seen. It also helped him keep cozy with agents and managers who represented talent he might want to work with. But in my case, the idea was that since an unrecognizable schmuck like me was lunching with a top player like Jennings meant that I must be 'somebody' too. Or at least a somebody to be. Guilt by association.

Jeff Lieberman • Day Of The Living Me!

It didn't take long for Jennings to figure out I was not impressed by these snobby pretentious grossly overpriced joints with their equally pretentious bullshit clientele of five foot agents and producers hopping from table to table with those fake hugs and kisses and promises to call with lines like 'Too long!' So one day when we were scheduled to 'do lunch,' Jane called to ask which restaurant I'd prefer and as she read off the usual list, Jennings butted in on the call.

'Lieberman, you don't give a fuck where we eat.'

"Not really, no."

"Good. Come to the studio and we'll go up to Fudruckers. I'm dying for a cheese burger!"

Fudruckers was a popular family restaurant at the top of the Universal lot, catering to the patrons of the Universal studio tours. So there we were, being shown to a table next to a birthday party outing of noisy kids. I loved hanging with this guy.

Over the next couple of months I was able to sell two other script idea projects, one to Norman Lear's Embassy Pictures and another to Warners, but it was easy for me to fit my *Mating Calls* re-writes in between them because they were so minor, sometimes only requiring an hour of my time. Jennings would get my re-write and get it off to the head of the studio, Sid Sheinberg, with just the changes earmarked for Sid's weekend read. Then on Monday I'd get Sid and Jennings notes. Sometimes it required even less than an hour of my time, but according to the writer's guild, any changes I made under the studio's direction was considered a 'draft,' and by guild contract I was to be paid ten thousand buckaroos each time. On the fourth draft Jennings asked me if I could drop a copy off at Sid's house in Belaire on my way home which I agreed to. I remember thinking, here I am acting like a messenger boy, slipping an envelope through the front gate of a mansion. But it didn't bother me at all because at least I was the highest paid messenger boy in history. As I headed back to my car I remember a stack of firewood in an adjoining driveway catching my eye and thinking, I've sure come a long way from stealing firewood to keep my family warm.

One day I was on the phone with Jennings discussing a re-write and he started rambling incoherently, not making any sense, jumping from subject to subject peppered in with something about getting medication at the drug store. I sensed something was wrong so I pretended to get another call and had to put him on hold. Then I dialed his number again and Jane picked up in the outside office.

Adventures of a Subversive Cult Filmmaker from the Golden Age.

"Jeff? You're on with Jennings."

"I am. I have him on hold. Can you see him?'

"His door's closed. What's wrong?"

"I dunno. Do me a favor, put me on hold and go in there. Pretend you left a pen or something. If he's okay, just come back and let me know."

She put me on hold. But she never came back on.

Later that afternoon Jane finally contacted me with a rundown of what transpired. When she entered Jenning's office he was slumped in his chair, head tilted back, his mouth open and eyes rolled back in his head. An ambulance came on the studio lot and took him to Cedars Sinai hospital where they diagnosed that he had suffered a major seizure.

The next day I went to visit him and when I entered his room he was sitting up in bed and greeted me with that same broad grin I came to expect. But sadly, his illness put an end to us making *Mating Calls*, and my chance to direct a studio movie. Though I was paid very well for our collaboration, my real payment was getting an inside look at the last of old Hollywood glamour.

P.S. Soon afterwards, Jennings suffered a major stroke and spent the next ten years unable to walk or speak, finally passing away in 1996. Years later his wife Monica Lewis wrote her autobiography and put the 'Jenning' vs. Jennings Hollywood rumor to rest. Though the incident occurred before she ever met Jennings, she assured her readers that the bullet missed Wanger's target by about two inches leaving a scar on Jenning's inner thigh, but both jewels were left in tact. As she points out, she should know.

21. IT'S AN ALIEN INVASION!

With the advent of home video ushering in the mid to late 80s period known as the "video invasion," more and more young people were exposed to *Just Before Dawn* as well as *Squirm* and *Blue Sunshine*.

It was an invasion in the sense that this foreign object, this plastic covered tape thingie containing movies inside was invading people's homes. I admit it was always a kick to see one of my titles on the racks at Blockbuster, Tower Video, Hollywood video and even Target. In fact, I used to hang out at places like Kim's video in Greenwich village were they had a shelf with my name on it, waiting to see if someone picked up one of my titles and then engage them in conversation.

It was during this period, at the height of the invasion, when I started to see these customers at the video store differently. A new generation of young people crowding into these stores, socializing and sharing their enthusiasm for movies and discovering sci-fi and horror movies like mine, made before they were even of movie going age or for some not even born yet. The words video invasion kept resonating in my brain. What was it about that phrase that hit me in such a strange way? Then I realized it was familiar because of the term "alien invasion." Then, just like that I asked myself the question, what if aliens are part of the video invasion? What if it's really an...

Once again it was time to take it to the yellow legal pad. Even though I could finally type at this point, I still relied on the trusty yellow pad to sketch out ideas in long hand.

"Aliens watched mankind evolve, waiting for them to advance technologically to the point that they'd invent the home video player and the cassettes that go with them, then use these earthlings' advances to destroy them…"

This time the government wasn't instilling fear on us. In fact they praised this new invention while movie theaters cursed it because they saw home video as a threat to their very survival. But what if it was also a threat to mankind's very survival? Then I tried to figure out how the aliens would go about achieving their goal. They'd have to somehow beam a signal to earth that would impregnate certain videotapes, then they could destroy us by remote control. *Remote Control* - I wrote that on the top of the page. It was a perfect title for this. What could be more remote than a distant alien planet and instead of controlling our programming they're controlling us!

The idea harkened me back to the beloved 1950s sci-fi movies of my youth. As an homage to them I made the 'movie-within-a-movie' where the aliens contaminate an obscure, black and white, 1950s sci-fi flick now being released on home video. I used to love the way sci-fi films of that era predicted what life on earth would be like in the future and how comically wrong they turned out to be in most instances. But sometimes they came pretty close to what would actually transpire in the future. What if one of those movies predicted we'd have home entertainment by the 1980s? The writers of 1950s sci-fi wouldn't be able to predict the exact advanced technology so they'd apply the tech they already had which was movie reels. But movie reels packaged inside a giant case that you rent and take home. Then it hit me, what if that was the very plot of this mythical sci-fi movie? And what if I called THAT movie *Remote Control* as well? And what if it had the same plot as what I was dreaming up? In fact, what if the aliens got the freaking idea of how to destroy mankind from that old movie in the first place!?

I scribbled this all down, and then drew a thick underline beneath that last sentence because I knew that one of the protagonists who invariably figures out what's going on in sci-fi movies should blurt out that line. The plot of some old sci-fi movie these evil alien beings were somehow able to see, gave them the idea of how to destroy mankind, so they decided to impregnate their signal within that very movie.

The rest came to me fast and furiously. The natural setting for this story was a video store, and the natural main character would be a video store clerk. He'd be the hero who figures all this out and must race against time to save mankind.

This was 1987 when studios realized that home video was a big insurance policy against box office failure. The new revenues pouring in made movie making, if not safe, then much less risky, especially with action or horror titles that didn't depend on a lot of dialogue because the video boom was happening all around the world.

If an actor had a recognizable name, known for anything at all, their value shot up because the "name on the box" became crucial to point of sale. I saw this first hand watching the crowds in video stores whose first question about any movie they weren't already familiar with was "who's in it?"

So a trick the smaller studios and independents picked up was to get the "almost" stars. Actors and actresses with famous siblings, or parents, similar to my casting Chris Lemmon for *Just Before Dawn*.

Based on a quick treatment I just as quickly made a writer-director deal with a new company headed by producer Herb Jaffee that was financed primarily to feed the exploding home video pipeline. So it was in that context of 'name on the box' casting that young actor Kevin Dillon was suggested to me for the lead role of Cosmo, the video store clerk. Though he was a virtual unknown at the time, his brother, Matt Dillon, was a second-tier star so the Dillon name on the box would actually mean something in publicity and point of purchase.

I had been impressed with Kevin's work in Oliver Stone's *Platoon* and agreed to let him play the lead role. I also wrote a sidekick role, Georgie the store's manager and Cosmo's boss. After Kevin was on board he urged me to see his friend who also had a small role in *Platoon* for the part of Georgie. Wanting to get off on the right foot with Kevin I added his friend to the casting list. When he came in to read, he was very shy and nervous and frankly bored me with his reading.

That night I was scanning through videotapes of the day's casting sessions when my now teenaged daughter passed behind me.

"Ooh, who's that?"

"Kevin's friend. Johnny something."

"He's cute. I'd go see the movie just for him!"

"You would?"

Maybe everyone reading this would too since Johnny Depp became a huge star and if you saw that one of his early movies was playing on HBO or Netflix you'd see it just for him. To this day, my daughter never misses an opportunity to remind me that I should have listened to her infinite teenage wisdom.

I did cast Jennifer Tilly as a local movie geek who frequents the video store and winds up renting *Remote Control* to her peril. At the time Jennifer's

Adventures of a Subversive Cult Filmmaker from the Golden Age.

only "name on the box" value came from being the sister of actress Meg Tilly. I rounded out the cast with a knockout beauty named Deborah Goodrich in the role of Kevin's love interest. Her polished sophistication made for great chemistry against Dillon's blue-collar crudeness. Ironically, Kevin's fame from the HBO series *Entourage*, and Jennifer's stardom from working with Woody Allen, along with headlining in the *Chuckie* franchise, boosted both of their "name on the box" values equal to their siblings.

Now in the 2Ks there's hardly any boxes to put names on anymore. Physical media is in its last days as streaming has taken over as the basic delivery system for all entertainment.

As for the movie *Remote Control*, although I was doing a satire of the times, which always calls for some exaggeration to make sociological points, it didn't seem to work that way for the audience who took it all way too literally. However, decades later that whole generation who grew up in video stores in the 80s and were introduced to their favorite movies through VHS, began waxing nostalgic about the home video of their youth and that resulted in Remote Control enjoying a very popular second life. Ironically, the exaggeration of that era now works perfectly as a sort of time capsule, both of the late 1980's and the home video revolution and the movie plays to enthusiastic sell out audiences everywhere I screen it.

22. WRITERS WRITE

For the next three years I shifted my focus to non-genre mainstream projects and with my screenwriting chops coming into full bloom, I cooked up an idea that was set in the future, centered around an eighty something baby boomer in a high end nursing home who through a semi realistic event finds himself traveling back in time to the 1980s and coming face to face with his younger self. I envisioned the same actor playing both roles and my number one pick to pull it off was Dustin Hoffman. Fortunately, playwright Murray Schisgal, who wrote the original script for *Tootsie*, was running Punch Productions, Dustin's production company. Murray knew of me from my working with Lansbury and Buruh so he was receptive to a pitch meeting. He instantly responded to the idea and saw it as a potential tour deforce for Dustin. Then the next day he called and invited me to come in and pitch to the actor himself.

Pitch a movie to Dustin Hoffman? Holy shit!

Fate would have it that I had already met the star, that is if my unique encounter can be considered 'meeting' him.

It was some time back in 1981 and I was having lunch with my then agent at the time, Irv Schwartz, at The Russian Tea Room in NYC. Seated at a table for two, Irv and I were deep in conversation when suddenly this obnoxious, homely woman rams into my chair while circling behind me to another table. Unapologetic she barges in on someone at another table while holding out a piece of paper and pen to get an autograph and sure enough it was Jon Voight she was pestering. A bit embarrassed and I'm sure pissed off, Voight scribbled on the woman's paper then turned back to his lunch plate.

Irv and I couldn't believe how obnoxious this woman was and wondered

Adventures of a Subversive Cult Filmmaker from the Golden Age.

how in hell they even allowed her in a classy place like the Tea Room.

Then the woman slid into a booth along side four other people and one of them waved to me and signaled for me to come over. I recognized the woman to be Renee Schisgal, (Murray's wife,) whom I'd casually known during her stint as an executive at Warner Brothers. Murray was at the table too and Renee did the intros, finally getting to the obnoxious woman.

"Jeff Lieberman, Dorothy Michaels."

Dorothy held her hand out to shake, then held onto my hand and said, "Jeff, you have such a firm firm grip. May I suck your cock?"

Then she broke this big grin that was very familiar to me and I realized who this was, fucking Dustin Hoffman in drag! He was deep into pre-production for 'Tootsie' and wanted to know if his character in drag would be convincing enough to the movie audience that they'd believe that the other characters in the film would believe she's a woman too. So what better place to try out his look and character than a popular restaurant where so many of his friends dined all the time. If they didn't recognize him, then nobody would question the validity of the character which was key to the movie's success. That explained why he tested it with Jon Voight, a close friend since working on *Midnight Cowboy* together.

Forward to eight years later as I arrived at the meeting at Dustin's Punch productions offices at the Time Life building in midtown. When I entered the conference room, Dustin was seated with his head leaned way back while a female assistant was applying eye drops for him.

"Hi Jeff, take a seat. This'll only take a second, but just hope she does this right because one little extra drop will blind me."

The assistant froze, then realized it was just another example of Dustin's sick humor and continued. I settled into a chair opposite him, then as an ice breaker, awkwardly offered, "We've met before."

"Really? Remind me."

I told him about our encounter that time at the Russian Tea Room when he was testing out his Tootsie role.

"...and when we shook hands you admired my firm grip, then asked if you could suck my cock."

Dustin sat up, blinked away the eye drops then extended his hand to shake, instantly transforming his voice and manner into the iconic Dorothy Michaels character.

"Well Jeff, so glad to see you again. And the offer still stands!"

That was one of the best meeting icebreakers I ever experienced.

Jeff Lieberman • Day Of The Living Me!

Big laughs all around. It put me completely at ease with this guy and I was able to slide into my A- game pitch mode. Dustin responded very positively to my idea and with him attached for the lead, the project was set up at TriStar Pictures. Like most scripts that get developed by a major studio, the writer gets paid, even when for whatever reason the movie never gets made. Murray's almost daily input upped my game immeasurably. His approach was to call me each afternoon and ask how I was feeling. That was his way of allowing me to vent any problems I was having without intruding on my creative flow. As a writer himself he knew that if I said I was feeling well it meant it was going well. And when I did offer where I was in the story he always reminded me to ask myself what each character wanted in every scene. Ulu Grosbard gave me the same advice about directing actors, that good actors are trained to know what their character wants right before they hear the word 'action.' I wished someone would've taught me all this shit from the beginning. There was actually a craft to all this!

A very strange thing happened while I was writing 'Us.' I'd find myself bursting into tears during certain emotional scenes. Sitting there all alone in an upper west side apartment I'd rented just for this one project, I'd be blubbering uncontrollably and with nobody around there was no reason to stop. It was the emotional core of the subject I was responding to, how a bitter old man gets a second chance to right the wrongs, heal the hurts he inflicted on loved ones and how it literally changes everything for him in his old age. The strangest thing was how, through Murray's guidance, the characters became so three dimensional, so real that I found myself just feverishly writing down what they said, almost like a court stenographer. Dustin himself has described that out of body experience in his acting- and tennis- referring to it as being 'in the zone.'

When I finished the first draft, Dustin, Tri-star and everyone at Punch Productions loved it. But Dustin being an insecure actor at heart, or just a very seasoned professional, take your pick, had to make sure he could attract a top Director to the project before fully committing to the role. He was shooting the movie *Hook* at that time and told Steven Spielberg about the storyline. Speilberg replied that it sounded just like *Back to the Future*, which I can see in a quick description but would never be the case had Dustin just given him the freaking script to read. Then Dustin approached Barry Levinson about it. They had struck gold with *Rainman* and were anxious to work together again. Hearing that Dustin would be playing an eighty something year old and a fifty something brought to mind that Dustin had told Barry that he hated sitting for

Adventures of a Subversive Cult Filmmaker from the Golden Age.

hours putting on make-up each day like he did on *Little Big Man* and then on *Hook*. He also pointed out that Dustin would be working in green screen to give the illusion that he was talking to his younger self, so really just working alone with nobody to play off.

That was it. Dustin was no longer attached for the lead role, but would be a producer. I knew right then it was over. Nobody cares if a star's name is listed on the producer credits if he's not in the movie.

However the screenplay did attract a lot of attention in Hollywood and I was quickly hired to write another script for *Rocky* Producer Robert Chartoff and Twentieth Century Fox. I had a great time getting to know Bob but alas, no movie came out of that either. Next I got hired to write one that actually did get made. It was a work-for-hire to write a third sequel to the family blockbuster *The Neverending Story*. I never even heard of it and wondered, "why me?" Since when did I ever write a children's fantasy story? My LA agents explained that something about my Dustin Hoffman script let my soft side leak through. A side I suppose didn't really resonate with worms crawling out of eyeballs or baby boomers freaking out on the after effects of LSD.

I was hired by the German movie producer Deiter Geisler who produced the original hit adaptation of the popular Michael Ende children's book. Deiter then did a sequel, *Neverending Story Two*, that got mostly negative reviews in the US where it made less than half the box office of the first one, but worldwide it did well enough to justify a third installment. That is, if they could do it for "a price," which is a Hollywood term for keeping the budget down to a bare minimum. That bare minimum was still in the tens of millions though, which meant my up front fee on this would be the biggest paycheck I ever got. And if I could manage to maintain sole credit on the script it'd be even bigger.

This was my first time writing something that wasn't my original idea. Not only that, but the source material was a children's book, an international best seller written by Michael Ende. My role was to breathe new life into the brand, but there were two big problems with this. First off, the international consensus of both critics and audiences was that the second movie didn't live up to the promise of the first, and some actually stated that they hoped this was the end of *The Neverending Story*. So despite all that, we were making a third with two strikes against us going in. The second thing was an even bigger problem, at least to me. The movie *Home Alone* had broken out so big, both in the states and internationally, that the entire industry seemed to have caught *Home Alone* fever. Everyone was desperate to tap into that same audience and Dieter and his German bankers were no exception. He wanted to make the movie more "Americanized," so that, along with me demonstrating a family-friendly mushy side, was why I got the job. Hire a red-blooded American and he'll automatically tap into the kind of societal quirks and pop references that helped make *Home Alone* a hit.

The original movie, and its predecessor centered around a mythical land called Fantasia where a large part of the movie took place. Not one thing contemporary about it and that was its charm. To make this version more like *Home Alone*, they wanted the characters to somehow come to the real world, which to them meant the American suburbs of the original movie (which was actually Vancouver, Canada).

I just knew this was all a huge mistake and no matter what I wrote it would be hated, both by the original fans of the first movie (which included most critics) and young parents who would eagerly want their kids to see the movie to show them what their childhood was like.

Working within those parameters I went at it and eight weeks later turned in a screenplay that triggered a green light from Dieter's German financing with the provision that they cast someone with a bankable name for the lead. Since the lead character, Bastian, was only twelve years old there were not a lot of choices and MacCauly Calkin was out of the question, already wrapped up for *Home Alone Two*. A movie called *Free Willy* was about to be released and Deiter's studio connections at Warners told him it was going to be a big hit and that Jason James Richter, the movie's young unknown lead, would be made into an overnight star. So Deiter rolled the dice and signed up young Jason for way more money than he earned on *Free Willy* hoping to cash in on its success. This crapshoot paid off with *Free Willy* shooting to the number one movie all around the world. Suddenly young Jason was a star.

Though I had nothing to do with the actual production of *Neverending Story Three*, I was contractually obliged to be present up at the Vancouver location to attend the table readings and make script tweaks with dialogue and also make adjustments for the actual locations that were chosen. But after things got rolling, most of my time was spent as an observer. I loved talking to the Henson Creature shop people, first founded by the great Jim Henson. It was my first glimpse into the world of animatronics and these folks were the best in the world. It was truly a joy to see my character the 'Bark Troll' come to life, with a puppeteer inside of him controlling his basic movements and another puppeteer yards away watching a monitor and controlling facial expressions remotely.

I also struck up a friendship with one of the cast members playing the role of the lead villain I created, a tough school bully named 'Slip.' By that point I was able to recognize actor's qualities and potential for stardom and this guy had the "it" factor. You just wanted to watch him during the shooting. If there were three or four other people with him, you still focused on him. Even when someone else was talking you were compelled to watch him listen. Reminded me of a young Jack Nicholson, and even more so a thinner version of John Belushi.

One night he and I we went out for burgers and beers at a nearby shopping mall. Whip smart and funny as hell, he confided that he was getting discouraged with his career and considering dropping out of acting to work full time with his band, which only consisted of one other person. My advice to him was to gain twenty pounds and be that fat guy, that Belushi, that John Candy, that guy with the mischievous edge Hollywood is always looking for comic relief.

I'd like to believe he took my advice but if it wasn't mine, then either someone else told him the same thing or he arrived at it on his own. In any case when Jack Black broke out big as that wacky, edgy, fat guy it was no surprise to me at all.

Oh, *The NeverEnding Story III* not only bombed but elicited such a steady stream of hateful outrage from the legion of fans who grew up on the original movie that I expected death threats. But most of the venom was aimed at the producers and the Director, Peter MacDonald, for that overt attack on their childhood. This was one time being "only the writer" really paid off.

23. BUT...SERIOUSLY

By 1993 my brain was fried from jumping from one Hollywood writing assignment to another. I had banked enough money to take a break and maybe do something different, preferably something that didn't require much writing. At least of the fictional kind.

Aside from 1950s sci-fi movies, the other obsession I had as a kid was Stand-up comedy, beginning with Bob Newhart and his debut LP *The Button Down Mind*. As I got older I started gravitating to the comics who focused on political and social issues of the so-called baby boomer years. It occurred to me that much of our history, what is generally accepted as truth in our historical narrative, was first defined by those stand-ups, not the mainstream news.

Not that the news outlets were lying to us. In fact, to the contrary, they were reporting the facts the best they could, unlike today where legions of so-called newscaster 'journalists' present their biased, cocktail party level opinions in the guise of news. The anchors that came before the introduction of cable -- people like Walter Cronkite, Harry Reasoner, Howard K. Smith, Chet Huntley and David Brinkley, read from their monitors without a hint as to who they voted for nor what their political leanings were.

But the words they spoke always had built into them the bias of the government who relayed the official "word from Washington," the '"word from the Pentagon" or "word from The White House," etc., which of course was spun with political propaganda favoring the party in power.

Whether they smelled bullshit or not, none of those prestigious nightly news hosts ever broke character and revealed their personal two cents. That was not their job. That wouldn't be news. It would be their opinion. Sounds

Adventures of a Subversive Cult Filmmaker from the Golden Age.

simple doesn't it?

So it was left to performers like Mort Sahl, Lenny Bruce, Richard Pryor and George Carlin to call bullshit for them. And for us. And not from any particular partisan point of view either. Like the newscasters, there was no telling who they voted for nor which political party they leaned toward. They were equal opportunity offenders and their commentary crossed all political and social lines. They were my heroes and I looked to them as soothsayers, the prophets of my time. Then I realized their opinions turned out to be the actual news after all. With 20-20 hindsight, the truths we've all accepted about the Vietnam war, racism, women's rights etc, were first articulated by those comics, not the mainstream news.

How could I prove that? If I could show what the news told us, say 40 years ago, then also show what the comics said about those very topics at that time, then repeat this process over and over year after year up to the present, it'd be clear it was the comics who were more right than wrong throughout modern history.

I had to pick a start date and settled on 1960 because it was around the time I became conscious of this stuff and also because up to then stand-up comics limited their material to mother-in-law jokes, marriage, and bratty kids, without a hint of social commentary until the new decade of the 60s ushered in the radical new approach of Mort Saul and Lenny Bruce. And it's a good thing it all started then because getting footage of comics before that would've been impossible since, by and large, it didn't exist. Nobody brought film camera crews and lights into smoky nightclubs before the sixties. I scribbled down a working title, *But Seriously*, that go-to refrain comics used to follow up a punch line and segue into another bit but used here to connote the emphasis on the serious side of making people laugh.

I thought this thing could make a hell of a documentary. But I'd been around long enough to know that such a massive undertaking would require a shit load of money. The rights issue alone would account for more than half the budget.

My friend and associate Fred Berner did his best to find a way to get financing but it soon became clear that there was no way any private source was going to put up that kind of money for a documentary, a form that had very little potential for return at that time. It would take a big company to take on the financial risk and recoup their investment either with commercial advertising or paid subscriptions.

Dead in the water, my only hope was to find a Rabbi to help make this happen so I put together a list of possible candidates, starting off with Rob Reiner. Since I couldn't think of anyone better for it, it was a very short list. Problem was, I didn't know him.

I did know Richard Crystal who I had cast in *Blue Sunshine* before he made the switch from acting to producing. Richie and I maintained a friendship over the years and always talked about doing something together and since his brother Billy was close with Rob, I figured Richie could make the connection I needed. I laid *But Seriously* on him and he got it right away. We agreed to be producing partners and if we got it set up with Rob's help, I would direct.

Three days later we were at Castlerock Entertainment's Beverly Hills headquarters and in Rob's office for the pitch. Rob listened intently, nodded then asked, "Who's the filmmaker?" I told him I was. Then he reiterated, "And you're going for the truth." We both nodded. Rob nodded. Then came his verdict, "How much you need?" We actually didn't know and took the next few days putting together a budget. With Castlerock riding high with Seinfeld, and Rob himself on top after his directing the academy award nominated *A Few Good Men*, the timing couldn't have been better. After a breakfast pitch to Showtime's Steve Hewett (son of Don Hewitt of '60 Minutes' fame) attended by Rob, me and Richard, the Network signed on with more than enough money to make the show we envisioned. Though Rob would be billed as Executive Producer, he made it clear it was Richard's and my baby and he'd seldom be around because he was starting production on a new movie called *North*. So with carte blanche from both Castlerock and Showtime, Richard and I were able to do the show without any interference, which was actually a bit intimidating. It was all on us to pull this monster thing off.

One by one the comics came on board, first Whoopie Goldberg and Robin Williams, then branching out to George Carlin, Richard Pryor, and Mort Sahl, until everyone with a stand-up act that centered on political and social issues wanted to be part of it. When the show was completed Castlerock and Showtime were very pleased with the finished product. So were the critics who had all been given advanced copies. Showtime started taking out full page trade ads with a tagline extolling, "The Critics. The Conscience. The Voices of our times" and Castlerock went all in on a big premiere showing at the Director's Guild of America Theater on Sunset boulevard.

The night of the premiere, JoAnn got all dolled up for the big night and I was so excited I almost wore a tie. When we arrived the place was packed.

Adventures of a Subversive Cult Filmmaker from the Golden Age.

It seemed like everyone in the world of comedy showed up. Many of them had nothing to do with the show, like Jerry Seinfeld and Bette Midler. Then there were others that did appear in it, like Billy Crystal, Mort Sahl, Pat Paulson and Lily Tomlin. CNN, Entertainment Tonight and other media were also scattered around with their cameras and lights to cover the event. JoAnn and I stood there gawking at all this and reacted the same way we did at the sight of that sea of humanity back at Woodstock, "Holyyyy shit!"

Then word got to me that Richard Pryor was in the house and my knees went weak.

"Pryor? Here? Where!"

JoAnn and I were led to a private VIP room where Richard sat in his wheelchair. I approached him and took his hand and just held on to it. His expression was lifeless, the drug induced burning incident coupled with the degenerative effects of multiple sclerosis had really taken its toll. I leaned in close to him and asked,

"How you feelin' man?"

"Oh, I got good days and bad days."

"What's today?"

"Bad day."

Fuck, he's having a bad day but came out for this anyway? I awkwardly posed for a picture with him then bowed out like some peasant who just got a minute's face time with the king.

The Director's Guild theater was packed, all 600 seats filled. Had a bomb gone off it would've been the end of comedy in America as we knew it. I had an aisle seat with JoAnn seated beside me, right behind Rob's parents, Carl and Estelle Reiner. As the lights dimmed I twisted around to scan for more celebrity faces one last time and noticed Pryor in the aisle one row behind me still in his wheel chair.

About fifteen minutes into the movie there's a piece that tackles poverty in the big cities during the civil rights struggles of the 1960s and we chose Pryor's rendition of "Nobody Wants You, When You're Down and Out," to play over it, then we cut to Richard himself as a young comic continuing performing the song before a small nightclub audience. It's a very powerful sequence and reveals an aspect of his talent very few people were aware of, his great belting blues voice.

When it ended the entire audience exploded in applause and I twisted around to see that Pryor was crying. I leaned back toward him and whispered, "That bad Rich?"

And he cracked up laughing which produced even more tears. For me too. In two seconds I had made Richard fucking Pryor cry and laugh. It does not get better than that.

When the end titles rolled the audience applauded enthusiastically. But this was not a civilian audience. These were all invited guests. And this was Hollywood where everyone in general is full of shit. So I started getting paranoid about whether they actually liked it or were just being polite. JoAnn assured me they all loved it but she's a trusting soul and I'm not.

Castlerock threw a big catered after party in the main lobby with plenty of food and drink. I spotted producer Marvin Worth standing to the side looking inconspicuously conspicuous with his long grey braided ponytail and custom-made Versace buckskin, tasseled Native American style suit. Among other things in his storied career, Marvin was Lenny Bruce's manager, along with Charlie Parker, Bette Midler and even Malcom X, so to me he was the hippest man in show business - and the only one who could get away with an outfit like that. I went over to him and asked timidly, "So? What do you think?"

"What do I think? I think what they think."

He pointed over to the smorgasbord line which was getting longer and longer by the minute, looking like a line at a high-school cafeteria, only these were major celebrities holding those trays.

"How do you know what they think?"

Marvin looked at me like the answer was so obvious it didn't deserve a reply, but he replied anyway. "Every one of them can afford to eat in any restaurant in L.A. If they didn't like the movie they'd be half way out the parking lot by now. Me too. Nice job."

With that Marvin patted me on the back then walked off and grabbed a tray for himself and got on line behind the others.

What he said was dead on. I'd made many a mad dash to the parking lot after special invite screenings when I didn't like the movie and wanted to avoid a face-to-face confrontation with the filmmakers. Such a big crowd sticking around was their way of saying they dug it. Leave it to Marvin to point that out.

Then JoAnn came over to me. "Who was that you were talking to? Is he an Indian?"

"Marvin Worth."

"What'd he say?"

"You were right, they all dug it."

Then I turned around and there was Lily Tomlin. Lily appeared in several pieces throughout the film and wanted to congratulate me on the movie. All I could do was gush like a fan boy. "I can't believe this, my two comedy Gods right here in the same room, Richard Pryor and you. I mean Goddess."

She flashed that trademark big toothy grin and grabbed my face with both hands but instead of kissing me, she shoved her tongue halfway down my throat!

That would make a great #Metoo story and grounds for a lawsuit except for, A, it's way beyond the statute of limitations and B, my response would get it thrown out in court, which was, "I'm never gargling again!"

But Seriously aired on primetime on a Saturday night and was so successful Showtime asked us to do another one, which of course was impossible unless we waited for another thirty-five years of news to pass. So they settled for a one-hour year-end show we called *But Seriously '94*, and this time we hired all the comics to perform bits themed around that year's major news events with the idea that the show would air around New Year's Eve. We couldn't afford the top tier comics, but Richard Crystal and I did put together a great line up starring David Brenner, Richard Belzer, Joy Behar, George Wallis, Andrew Dice Clay and others.

Over the following twenty years, the advent of cable and 24-7 news channels competing for niche audiences resulted in the end of unbiased objective news as we knew it, both in newspapers and TV broadcasts. Now its crystal clear who every anchor voted for and what their political and social leanings are, facts are now interwoven with their commentary skewed to appeal to their niche audiences - exactly the way early television interwove their entertainment with their sponsor's messages. Ironically, now left without any source of actual unbiased news, a great portion of the public have turned to comedians for their facts. Not just their commentary, their opinions, their spin, their perspectives -- but the actual news itself!

Suddenly comics like Jon Stewart, Bill Maher, Joy Behar, Whoopie Goldberg, Stephen Colbert, people without any real world experience credentials at all in journalism, world affairs, politics, economics, the sciences or anything else other than comedy are now re-purposed as talk show hosts who pontificate before huge T.V. audiences. And they're even quoted daily in news publications as if they were elected officials. The unbiased, take-no-prisoners, non-partisan bullshit-calling comics of old have given way to largely one-sided material that attacks their perceived enemies and protects their own allegiances all designed to appeal to their niche audiences. The death knell of the topical comedy I embraced in my youth has rung.

Sometimes I wonder if I had anything to do with this phenomenon. Did our glorification of this brand of comedy in *But Seriously* play a role in the transformation of these stars from comedy club performers to fake news anchors? I hope it was all just part of the zeitgeist and would've happened anyway but I have reason to believe I contributed to it at least to some extent.

I'd love to see us return to the days of Cronkite, Huntley Brinkley and the others when news and commentary were as strictly separated as church and state. And comics went for the jugular of truth regardless of whose necks they had to bite to get to it.

But seriously…

With Richard Pryor,
But…Seriously premiere

Lily Tomlin,
But…Seriously premiere

24. HOWDY DOODY TAKES THE NIGHT TRAIN

1995 starts with a flash back. I usually hate flash backs because of the word "back," as in backwards, when a narrative is supposed to go forward. But in this case a flashback is key to the story:

FLASH BACK TO: July of 1962. My father took the family to the Pines Hotel in South Fallsburg, New York. The Catskills. The Borscht belt. The Jewish Alps. Complete with everything that entailed, the social scene, the "tummlers" working the sunbathers around the pools. Guests lined up for the all-inclusive breakfasts, lunches and dinners. Some of them ate everything on the menu, then mulled around in the lobby waiting to charge into the dining room for the next meal as if they feared the hotel might suddenly run out of food.

All of these Borscht Belt hotels had day camps for the kids, advertised as jam-packed with activities but their prime reason for existence was to get the kids out of their parents' hair so they could enjoy themselves with other adults. The Pines was no exception. But I was never big on camps of any kind, nor any organized youth activities for that matter. And besides, at 14, I thought I was way too old for that shit. So left to fend for myself in the hot summer heat, I wandered around the grounds and noticed what looked like a small circus tent. On closer inspection, I saw that it was an enclosed boxing ring, surrounded by speed bags and a huge heavy bag hanging from the rafters off to the side. As I drifted in closer, I heard music playing. Scratchy rhythmic music emanating from the tinny little speaker of a portable record player. It was James Brown's rendition of "Night Train."

Jeff Lieberman • Day Of The Living Me!

I peeked inside the tent and there jumping rope was this big black man, eyes closed, sweat shooting off him, skipping away to the beat. Then I noticed a sign. It read "Sonny Liston training camp, home of the night train."

Sonny Liston. I had heard that name before. Up until then I had only a moderate interest in boxing, my exposure limited to watching the Friday night fights with my Grandpa Dave. Brought to you by Gillette, with Don Dumphey at the mic. I knew Floyd Patterson had beaten Ingemar Johansson and regained his heavyweight title, but I had no idea I was in the presence of his next contender. I kept drifting in closer, drawn by the music and the sound of leather hitting leather. I'd never seen anything like this before. Then a very nice looking black woman called out to me, "Come sit down!' and she patted the empty chair next to her.

I sat down and marveled at Sonny doing a headstand, with two trainers holding him for balance so he could keep his arms flat at his sides while his entire two-hundred-twenty pound weight was supported by the strength of his neck! Then he bent his head to one side, then the other. I could hardly watch, but I couldn't turn away either.

"What's your name?" the woman asked.

"Jeff…"

"Jeff, I'm Geraldine. And that there's my husband, Sonny. Anyone ever tell you you look just like Howdy Doody?"

Actually, yes, Jayne Mansfield did. But you'll learn about that later on. I still had those freckles that blossomed in the summer and still parted my hair in a straight line, front to back and plastered it down with that pasty schoolboy hair tonic everyone used back then.

"I know. People call me that all the time."

"Well that's good. That's cute. All them big freckles and all."

I didn't think it was so cute because I didn't want to be cute. I was in the midst of discovering girls and I wanted them to think I was handsome, not cute. It would take me decades to learn the simple fact that girls, even grown women, use the word cute to describe pretty much anything they like, especially when it pertains to anything about members of the opposite sex.

Now this giant of a man was heading right toward us, wiping a torrent of sweat from his brow.

"Sonny, this is Jeff. Don't he look like Howdy Doody?'

Sonny broke a huge toothy grin and in an instant this gigantic, evil-looking, brooding, scary man transformed into a warm, friendly guy. I shot out of my chair so he could sit next to his wife.

150

Adventures of a Subversive Cult Filmmaker from the Golden Age.

"No, no, that's okay. Room for both of us."

I slid over to make way and found myself wedged between them like the cream in an Oreo cookie. He put his arm around me and gave me a squeeze.

"Howdy Doody. You like boxing?"

Well, I sure did now. I felt instantly comfortable with this man, just like I did with my father's friends. In fact, he smelled like J&B, which was the stuff my dad drank on special occasions. And which some of his friends drank when the occasion wasn't so special. I identified that familiar odor instantly, not that it was Scotch, but that is was a particular brand of Scotch which decades later I would learn was indeed Sonny's brand of choice. I'd also learn that it was NOT common to smell that way in the middle of the afternoon, in the middle of a training session for a shot at the heavyweight championship of the world.

Sonny sat with me for all of a minute, the time a fighter gets to recover on his stool between rounds, then someone yelled "Time!" which was Sonny's cue to get up and get back to action, working the speed bag, skipping rope, hitting the heavy bag, everything done in three-minute increments, the exact time of a round of boxing. And there was this guy, this old timer, sporting a straw stingy brim and a toothpick embedded in the side of his mouth. His job was to lift the arm of the record player and set it back down at the beginning of the record, each time exactly as the next round began. James Brown.

"All aboard, the Night Train!'

And so it went for several more rounds, Sonny returning to my seat between each round. During one round, Sonny hit that heavy bag so hard it yanked the eyehook right out of the plywood frame and the bag went crashing to the floor. All I could think was, what happens when he hits someone in the jaw like that?

Then I realized nearly two hours had passed and my parents were probably looking for me. So I said goodbye to Geraldine and Sonny, and headed back to the hotel.

That night, in the main dining room, I was seated at the kid's table along with my brother and several of my parent's friend's kids. I was bored because all they talked about was that stupid camp they went to while I was doing something so cool. Of course at that time I couldn't grasp its import and the impact it would have on my adult life.

Off across the expansive room, I saw a group of black men being led to a table at the far side of the dining room. One of the kids spotted them too. "Hey, that's Sonny Liston. My father says he's training here."

Then this other kid digs his fork into a slab of meat on his plate, and holds it up toward Sonny.

"Here Sonny, eat! Good!"

I was humiliated. Sonny could see me sitting with these stupid morons so he must've thought I'm one of them. The right thing to do would have been just to knock the kid out right then and there. But what I actually did was turn around and hide my face. I was so ashamed. Ashamed to be sitting at this table. Ashamed that color meant everything to so many people and that these jerks defiantly got this shit from their parents. That moment solidified my thinking about human nature for all my adulthood. I was embarrassed by it. Humiliated. I was not one of them. I wasn't white. I wasn't Negro. So around most people I was just some sort of outsider. And I'd much rather have been sitting with Sonny and Geraldine than these idiots. I just didn't have the balls to actually get up and do that. But it did help me clarify who I was at a critical juncture of my life so for that I thank that stupid little bastard.

About three weeks later I was back in Valley Stream, walking with a bunch of guys toward the shopping mall. When we reached the main intersection of Sunrise Highway, a policeman was holding back automotive and pedestrian traffic for some official reason. Then a couple of police motorcycles with flashing lights appeared followed by a lone black guy, hood over his head, jogging with his head down.

"Who's that?" asked one of the kids.

The cop turned to us and shouted, "Floyd Patterson. Get a good look kids, the heavyweight champion of the world!"

I got a good look all right. And all I could think of was Sonny ripping that heavy bag out of the plywood and imagining what one of those punches, just one, would do to this little guy.

"Sonny's gonna kill this guy with one punch." There it was, my very first fight prediction and of course I turned out to be right.

FLASH FORWARD TO 1994. Sonny made such an impression on me at such a pivotal time in my life that when I learned of his untimely death in 1970, I became more and more interested in the details of his life and how suspicious the circumstances of his death seemed to be. Finally, sometime in 1994 I pitched a bio documentary on Liston to Ross Greenberg, Senior Vice President of HBO Sports at the time. The timing was perfect riding on the documentary chops I displayed in But Seriously and to his credit,

Adventures of a Subversive Cult Filmmaker from the Golden Age.

Ross got the import of Sonny's story immediately. Just like that I was off and running to retrace every detail of Sonny's life as well as the mystery surrounding his sudden death.

That quest eventually led me to St. Louis, and Geraldine Liston's doorstep. After Sonny died, Mrs. Liston left Las Vegas and all that life entailed and returned to her birthplace to live with her mother. That was the house she was still living in over twenty years later when she accepted our request for an interview.

Geraldine looked very much as I remembered her, only much older and grayer, of course. I helped her into a chair in the dining room and then sat down right in front of her in official interviewer's position. While the crew busily set up the camera and lights all around us, I had a little chat to put her at ease about the kinds of questions I'd be asking and stressing that the furthest thing I want to do is portray Sonny in the negative light that pretty much everyone had done up to that point in time. In fact, George Foreman refused to participate in the film. George had sparred with Sonny when George just turned pro and Sonny was his idol and he assumed this would be just another smear of Sonny, the criminal, the big ugly bear.

I moved in closer to Geraldine and asked,

"Do you remember when Sonny trained at the Pines hotel for the first Patterson fight? 1962?" Geraldine thought a minute, then replied, "Yes, the Pines. That's right, uh huh. Nice place."

"Do you remember a white boy sitting with you watching Sonny train?"

She reached back into her memory bank, but wasn't coming up with anything.

"Howdy Doody?"

Another few beats and her eyes lit up.

"Howdy Doody! Yes! But... how do *you* know that?"

I locked eyes with her. This was fucking great...

"Cause I'm Howdy Doody!"

"Oh Lord! Oh lordy, lord!"

She got up and hugged me and I hugged her and the two of us started crying with joy while the flummoxed crew had no idea what the hell was going on.

In our research for the film we learned that Sonny and Geraldine were trying to have children but for whatever the reason could not. They both loved kids, especially Sonny, so it could have been any kid sitting in that chair at his training camp that summer day in the Catskills and he probably would've reacted the same way. In fact after Sonny lost the title to Ali he fought over in Sweden where he and Geraldine adopted a white boy. Being Swedish, I doubt the kid looked anything like Howdy Doody, but I'll bet they loved him just the same.

The following year the HBO documentary *Sonny Liston; the Mysterious Life and Death of a Champion* won three EMMY awards including mine for producing and directing. The EMMY trophy sits right next to George Burns' cigar, slowly decaying in its glass tube. Just like me...

The Jeff Howdy Doody

The real Howdy Doody

25. DAY OF THE LIVING ME

The success of *But Seriously* and the Sonny Liston documentary placed me right in the thick of the "non-scripted" boom that was emerging in the mid-nineties. Between that and my screenplay for *The Neverending Story III* being produced, I was firmly ensconced in Hollywood, living the good life in a large Spanish style house in Beverly Hills with no financial worries at all. One day I got a phone call from New York, a guy named Michael Gingold who introduced himself as a staff writer for something called *Fangoria*. I had never heard that name before and when he started talking about *Squirm* I figured it was some prank from one of my friends. My early work, *Squirm*, *Blue Sunshine* and *Just Before Dawn* were distant memories at that point. In fact, nobody but my agent even knew I made those movies. Horror in general was not on the Hollywood radar at all, and there was no upside in even bringing it up as a credential. So why was this guy calling me? He told me *Fangoria* was a horror and sci-fi fan magazine, and the readers would be very interested in an interview with me. I questioned how they even knew who I was let alone that I made those movies, and he said a small portion of them saw the films in movie theaters when they were young, but the majority discovered them on either television or home video. I was blown away by the idea that there was even a small cult group of people from the next generation who knew me from those films. I agreed to do an interview with Mike next time I was in New York and he gave me a date to consider which would coincide with a *Fangoria* convention held in midtown Manhattan.

Around a month later my family was in New York for a visit and I took my fourteen-year-old daughter Emily along with me to the Fangoria convention at the New Yorker hotel. I couldn't imagine what in hell a horror convention would be like. Conventions to me meant guys in suits with plastic nametags and drinks in their hands grab-handing one another with big phony grins. So when we got off the elevator we were both in for a big surprise. No suits and no nametags, that's for sure. Some people wore horrific costumes emulating their favorite horror films, but the common attire was black tee shirts featuring horror imagery from their favorite movies, the most common among those were from George Romero's *Night of the Living Dead* and *Day of the Dead*.

Emily was awestruck. This was Halloween on a winter's day. And mostly adults, which made it pretty frightening for her. Then she saw something that made her jaw drop in awe.

"Oh my God! The Misfits!"

I looked over to where a group of hard-core costumed rockers were signing autographs and posing for pictures with their fans. I had no idea who they were but it was clear they had an enthusiastic fan base, which included my daughter, who was deep into metal at the time.

"I can't believe it's them. Think they'll let me get a picture?"

"Sure. I'll go ask."

I dug out a digital camera from my bag and went over to them to ask. The Misfits were very polite and accommodating, a direct contrast to the black leather, chains and scary make-up they were wearing. One of the leaders, Jerry Only, asked Emily how old she was and when she told him he said there's not many kids there, it's sorta just for adults. She explained she was there with her dad who would be speaking or something about his movies.

"Who's your dad?"

"Jeff Lieberman."

He and the others looked over at me.

"Jeff Lieberman? Like *Squirm* and *Blue Sunshine*? That's him?" One of them called over to me, "Mister Lieberman, after you get this, can we get a shot with you?"

"Sure," I said, completely taken by surprise. I never heard of them but they heard of me? How could this be?

Emily was more than shocked as she watched their assistant come over to get a picture of them posing with me. Then when she asked Jerry for his autograph he said only if she would autograph something for him. It made her feel important being my daughter, which was really sweet of him.

I wondered how many others among these throngs know who I am

Adventures of a Subversive Cult Filmmaker from the Golden Age.

from those movies? No way of knowing because nobody knew what I looked like. After passing table after table stocked with horror related paraphernalia and videotapes I finally found the *Fangoria* table and met Mike Gingold. He was an affable guy over twenty years my junior, closer to my older daughter Erika's age, as were the majority of the fans at that convention. Mike being a big horror fan himself seemed very excited to meet me in the flesh, shake my hand and recount when and where he first saw *Squirm* and how it inspired him to immerse himself in the genre. Then he started introducing me around. As the word spread that I was there, a mostly male, goth-themed fan base I didn't know started converging from every direction. I grabbed Emily's hand tight to make sure she was at my side. It was like we suddenly found ourselves inside of a new horror movie called *Day of the Living Me*!

They started asking for my autograph, which seemed so weird to me that I didn't want to do it. Why? Who am I, Micky Mantle? I never understood why people wanted autographs of celebrities anyway. A picture with them, sure, but not autographs. I did get one celebrity autograph way back when I was that ten year old, freckle-faced kid. And it was one time those freckles really paid off.

It was at the Coconut Grove nightclub in the Ambassador hotel in Hollywood in the late 1950's. My father was running a charity function for the City of Hope and the iconic art deco nightspot was packed with celebrities. My brother and I were the only kids there and were more taken with the dozens of palm trees growing all around the club than the event of the evening. We'd never seen indoor trees before, let alone palm trees. As far as celebrities go, I only recognized one of them, Pinky Lee, who was one of my TV favorites at the time. I couldn't believe he was there in person. And in color! My parents gave me a piece of hotel stationary and a pen and led me over to Pinky to get his autograph. He was a very nasty man and with his signature lisp complained that my pen didn't work right and made me feel like I was just bothering him. I backed away and then when I turned around I was suddenly face to face with boobies! The biggest ones I'd ever seen. And the woman who owned them was gorgeous. Bleached blonde and glamourous, clutching the arm of a big handsome muscular man.

"Look Mickey," she said, "its Howdy Doody!"

In order to pinch my cute cheeks this blonde goddess had to bend down to my height, which caused her low cut dress to flop forward enough for me to get a glimpse of two of the most majestic breasts ever seen by mankind!

Jeff Lieberman • Day Of The Living Me!

When someone asked her for her autograph it was clear she was famous for something so I asked for one too. I held out my pen and paper and she bent down again and scribbled it for me, "With love, Jayne Mansfield," dotting the letter i with a heart.

I ran back to show this treasure to my parents and they explained that Jayne was indeed a movie star and the muscle guy was her husband body builder Mickey Hargitay.

"I'm getting another one!" I ran off to get a second eyeful because truth be told, ten-year-old me wasn't really interested in another autograph.

So back to that Fangoria convention and here I was being treated like some kind of celebrity. And to the Fangoria crowd I actually was. While Emily stood by I posed for photo after photo. When I finally led Emily away to see the rest of the convention I realized a lot of the fan group was following behind us. I had an entourage! This was so unexpected that I couldn't really process it at the time. There was a whole new world out there I was totally unaware of. A new appreciation for the horror genre and the people who defined the modern versions of it in the 1970's, me being among them. The others had much bigger name recognition, John Carpenter, George Romero, Toby Hooper and Brian DePalma. With the exception of DePalma they all spent their careers exclusively in the horror genre while I veered as far away as you can get, but I was nevertheless grouped in with them based on the re-discovered work of my youth. The thing that resonated with me the most was my sudden relevance to the younger generation. Back when I made those movies it never occurred to me that anyone would be watching them even a year or two later, let alone thirty-five years later. And not only watching them but seeing something historically important in them for a new generation of fans. This made me feel sort of younger myself. I got a surge of energy that had been lying dormant. It was an unexpected revelation and it took me a long time to process, but it certainly was my Day of the Living Me.

26. SATAN HELPS ME COPE WITH THE BIG FIVE-OH

1997. As Bob Dylan sang around that time in his tune *Mississippi*, "Things should start to get interesting, right about now."

And a little scary also for me and my fellow legions of baby-boomers. The "duck drill" kids, the polio pioneers, the hippies, the yuppies, the "me generation," the "forever young" generation were about to turn 50 and were suddenly coming face to face with their own mortality. They called it midlife but the unspoken truth was that the only way that could be true was if you lived to a hundred. Otherwise you were rounding the far turn and headed into the home stretch of life.

I didn't really feel any particular crisis coming on, at least not attached to some round number of years I'd been in existence, but since my big five-oh birthday was in mid-October I thought it made for a perfect excuse to round up all my friends for a big Halloween costume party.

Halloween was always my favorite holiday. It was actually the only holiday I could relate to as a kid. All the religious ones were based on a load of ancient superstitions transformed into adult fairytales. So was Halloween for that matter but the celebration of the dead morphed into something else, something that profoundly revealed a fundamental fact about human nature. About who we really are. The way I saw it, most people were in costume 364 days of the year. They not only wore a costume every one of those days but behaved as the character in that costume was expected to behave. Like back when I threw my yellow writing pad aside and put on a jacket and tie to ride the train into Manhattan looking for a nine-to-five job. And when I found one at Janus, I became one of the herd of commuters engaging in small talk on the train platform every morning, saying things like "cold enough for ya?" in the winter and "hot enough?" in the summer. I behaved as my costume dictated, but it sure wasn't who I really was beneath it.

However, on this one day, October 31st, the chains of conformity were lifted and people were free to express their true selves instead of playing that fake persona they presented every other day of the year.

But even given this freedom, most people are reticent to really let go and reveal themselves, choosing safe costumes that are not really them, just trading one costume for another, like the cop out of choosing to dress as famous characters from movies or pop culture. They're so wrapped up in their every day costume and the persona that goes with it, that they can't handle making that big a transition to illustrating self expression while knowing they have to go back to their everyday costume the very next morning.

Then there are the few of who savor the liberation of taking off that forced societal costume. So, for me Halloween is the only time you can really know who everyone is, simply by their choice of costume. This is not to say that they actually need to wear a costume. Nor that the costume itself expresses who they really are. It's far more complex than that. There are people who will show up at a Halloween costume party without dressing up at all. But they're still in a costume of sorts because they come dressed as the character they've been playing all year, and they'll behave accordingly, their subtext being, "this is silly, go on and have your fun, I'll watch from the sidelines while you all make fools of yourselves." Then there are others who arrive in the most minimal costumes, like a simple eye mask, or bunny ears, just a token bow to the season, like wearing reindeer antlers at a Christmas party. This behavior falls into another personality type, going along with the crowd in the most non-committal way that won't draw any attention to themselves, which is exactly what they do every other day of the year.

There's also the women who take advantage of the holiday to show off their gym sculpted bodies in ways they'd never dare do on any other day by dressing as hookers, or sexy "cats." This overtly sensual exhibitionism speaks directly to who these women are, people who have been suppressing their sexuality to fit in with social mores when they really want to let it all hang out and scream "Get a load of me!"

But then there are the real Halloween people, the ones who wait for this one special day to come out of their self-imposed closet and give people a genuine glimpse of their true personalities, at what's really going on inside their brains every day. To show who they really are. And the costumes they put together have a huge impact on how they behave on Halloween. Think about all this the next time you're invited to a costume party and you ask yourself, "what am I gonna be?" Or better yet, when you arrive at the door and someone asks you "What are you supposed to be?" You'd better have an answer, at least for yourself. Which of these groups do you fall into? Which goes for me too. So, what was I gonna be for my big 50 extravaganza? I knew one thing. I shouldn't make any snap decisions. I learned that lesson the hard way back in --

LATE OCTOBER, 1979...

My friend Bruce Steiner, a hilarious six-foot six gay plumber extraordinaire, decided to throw a costume party for his friends at his Riverdale apartment. Bruce wanted everyone to make their best effort to come up with something fabulous so he emphasized there would be prizes for the best costume.

As soon as I read the invitation I knew what I'd be. It was easy. A no-brainer, I'd just come as one of the bald headed maniacs from the movie I made the previous year, *Blue Sunshine*.

Putting together the look would be easy. I'd just go out and find a baldhead costume kit, then slip on my old *taekwondo dobok* backwards to make it look like a straight jacket. Then all I'd have to do was widen my eyes and flail my arms maniacally for everyone to get the joke.

JoAnn's plan was to come as a "hippie" which was pretty close to her every day looks only a few years before this. She hauled a vintage long flowered dress out of the attic, slipped it on, then fitted on a black frizzy wig. Now it was my turn. She sat me down in the bathroom and started applying gum Arabic to my rubber skullcap, but I stopped her and said to use rubber cement instead because it's much stronger and was what the make-up people did on *Blue Sunshine*.

JoAnn made the switch, brushed the cement under the edges of the bald cap, then carefully placed the whole thing atop my head. I tapped it all around with my fingertips then nodded my approval.

"Now pull it way back so it covers my whole hairline like a shower cap, then press down the edges where the glue is."

With both hands she stretched the rubber all the way down to the top of my neck and pressed the edges down with her thumbs, while I held the front.

"Okay, now let go..."

Jeff Lieberman • Day Of The Living Me!

As soon as she let go the strength of that stretched elastic sprang up from all around my head, ripping away all the short hairs on the back of my neck, Brazilian wax style. The pain was unexpected and excruciating, like the time I was mowing my lawn barefoot, wearing nothing but a bathing suit and ran over a wasp's nest. Just like then I started flailing my arms and smacking the back of my neck like a maniac. A maniac in a straight jacket. So naturally JoAnn thought I was just doing character shtick from *Blue Sunshine*.

"The glue! Get it off me!"

"Why?!"

I had no time to explain, it was like my neck was on fire. The shower! I jumped in the shower to try to wash it off, but when I pulled at the back of the cap it hurt even more so I just dug my fingers into the center of my head and ripped the thing open. That relieved the pressure so I could peel away the rubber remnants and scrub off the glue.

When I stepped out of the shower we both had a good laugh. Then the realization hit us. The party was called for eight PM and it was seven o' clock already! Crap. That was my costume. What can I be? No time to put together another costume. Unless…

When in doubt, go in drag! Straight men dressing up as women had been a mainstay at every adult costume party I'd ever attended, and this one will surely have lots of gay men in attendance doing that also so that's what I'll be, a woman. Attending this party would be akin to the time Tony Macherella went full drag for the first time for his coming out party at Club 82. I'd play it real, just like De Niro would have.

First off I needed a wig and the only answer on such short notice was for JoAnn to give me hers, which meant she'd also have to come up with an alternate last minute costume. I told her I have some fake fangs in my office, maybe she can build something around that. While she went off to snatch the fangs, I fitted the huge black frizzy wig over my head and it immediately had a transformative effect.

JoAnn rushed in with the fangs, then climbed into the attic and emerged with one of her old maternity dresses, which should have been big enough to fit me, a long red cotton number. I wrestled into the dress while JoAnn started slapping make-up on her face. I asked her what she was gonna be?

"Don't know yet."

When she finished filling in her cheeks with dark shadow for that sunken dead look, she fitted the fangs in her mouth, then circled her lips with bright red lip stick, resulting in a cross between a ghoul and a vampire which was pretty cool.

Now it was my turn for the make-up kit.

When straight men dressed in drag for costume parties, they always made sure you knew they were still a manly man. So they'd put on tons of make-up with exaggerated red lips, giant balloons for boobs and a big cigar in their teeth.

But that's not what Tony Macherella did and I wouldn't either. I asked JoAnn to make me up the way she would if I were her girlfriend. This is what I look like, big frizzy hair, flat chested with a patch of black hair showing where my cleavage should be.

"Think of my beard as unwanted facial hair, as they say in the commercials. Cover it up the best you can. This is what you have to work with so make me look the best you can."

JoAnn giggled gleefully and went right to work. When she was done and I turned around to the mirror, it was one of the weirdest sensations I ever had. Even weirder than tripping on acid, because this was really happening! I'm looking at myself as a woman. My feminine alter ego. It really freaked me out.

I started to *act* like that woman in the mirror. Realizing it was chilly outside, I climbed into the attic then emerged wearing my mother's old mink stole and off we went, the ghoul and the drag queen motoring down the Henry Hudson Parkway to Riverdale.

Going to a party full of strangers and not exactly the bell of the ball, I acted insecure and clung to JoAnn's arm as we entered Bruce's apartment, glancing around to see if anyone was staring. It took a while for my friends to recognize me and when they finally did, one by one they went down like bowling pins, buckled over in laughter. The last to realize it was actually me, was one of my very closest friends. His face lit up and actually blushed, overtaken with the insanity he was beholding.

But they let me continue my character and actually started playing along. An older guy I didn't know sprung out of his seat and offered it to me. I thanked him profusely because those heels I was in were bloody hell. When the seat next to me opened up right beside his wife, he started playing kneezies with me! He had no idea who I was! I didn't know if this was due to the success of the costume or that he just had very peculiar taste in women, but I slapped his knee away making it clear I wasn't that kind of girl.

Oh, I won first prize for best costume.

Jeff Lieberman • Day Of The Living Me!

Cue the harp music and ripple dissolve back to:

1997, as my flashback ended with that depressing image in the mirror of my middle-aged mug staring back at me pondering what he should be for his fiftieth birthday party. The stark realization that Howdy Doody was just a distant memory, that the word 'cute' would never be used to describe that face again was very sobering to say the least.

If the experience of dressing up in drag exposed a side of me that I kept hidden all the other days of the year, what else have I been suppressing? Bang, it hit me, my age! Like Peter Pan I was refusing to grow up, which to me meant growing old.

So I went with old. I'm not talking turning fifty old, I mean nursing home old, a caricature of an old Jewish man in a bathrobe, slippers, ancient Bob Dylan tour tee shirt and rubber old man mask, complete with wild white hair. As soon as I got into this get up I started coughing up phlegm. The character just came naturally because I was playing ME in another thirty years.

CUT TO: THE NIGHT OF THE PARTY, pretty much everyone who was invited showed. And in costume. They were all relaxed and comfortable enough with each other to play out the characters they took on, which made for a rollicking party.

An hour or two later, the house was packed, people dancing, drinking and carrying on. I was dancing away in the living room when a guy in a fantastic gorilla outfit appeared. Either someone let him in or he just entered the front door unannounced but there he was, covered up by one of those full- body ape costumes you get from a costume rental. From his actions, the typical lug who goes around scaring the girls and pinching their asses, I immediately figured out who it was because it was definitely the suppressed personality trait of one of my friends who shall go unnamed.

Then the gorilla ape rolled his way over to the stereo, switched the music to his own disco CD, and started dancing with me. I was stoned and drunk so I had little choice but to go along with him. It wasn't easy keeping my equilibrium while being swung around in circles inside a bigger circle formed by the other party guests clapping along like it was the hora at a Jewish wedding.

Then I saw it. Something that sobered me right up, at least temporarily. The friend I thought I was dancing with was actually on the sidelines clapping along, dressed up as a worm-faced man in homage to my movie *Squirm*!

Shit, this was scary. I tried to clear my head. Who the hell was this? Everyone was accounted for. Could he be a party crasher? Or a robber?

Adventures of a Subversive Cult Filmmaker from the Golden Age.

Anyone could have shown up for this party, all they had to do is hear it was a costume party and know what time it started, then arrive fashionably late so they wouldn't get scrutinized by the hosts at the door. (So keep that in mind for next year, you can crash just about any Halloween party if your costume fully disguises your real identity and you show up about an hour late.)

Okay, now I was in a predicament. I asked Mister gorilla who he was but he just grunted and pretended not to understand. I started to panic. I searched for JoAnn in the crowd, trying to send out a signal that we could be in a 911 situation that very second! This guy could be here to empty our wallets, and maybe rob our house. He could even have other goons outside waiting for the all-clear signal!

Or... it could just be someone I forgot I invited. In the middle of all this, I got this funny sensation that I get whenever a new idea springs into my head. In this case, I didn't know where the idea would lead me but there was definitely something there, an evil person in a Halloween costume being mistaken for a trusted friend or family member and welcomed into a household with open arms. While mulling this over in the creative side of my brain, the rational side was in Defcon five mode, planning some sort of defensive move like tackling the guy or screaming for all my friends to rush him. What held me back was the fear of making a terrible and embarrassing mistake. Then the music suddenly stopped. This was it. He reached into a hidden pocket in his costume, which surely meant he was about to pull out a knife or a gun. But instead he pulled out a birthday card and announced,

"Happy birthday, from Charlie and Beth!"

It was a freaking gorilla-gram! Of course! How could I be so stupid? Actually, if it were any other day, I would've known that instantly. I mean, it's your birthday and a guy in a gorilla outfit ambles up to your front door? Might as well be a candy-gram. But on Halloween, that's a whole different set of apples. Ironically, our friends Charlie (you might remember him as the late actor Charles Rocket) and his wife Beth couldn't make it in from Los Angeles so they sent a gorilla gram, completely forgetting it was a costume party!

Well, at least a new idea had come out of it and I was curious to see where it took me as I let it ruminate in my mental hard drive over the next five years. It was the stark reality of that moment, the realization that this gorilla man could actually be a murderous intruder that stayed with me. The reality of that moment is what I'll never forget. Trying to find a story vehicle that would replicate that moment finally resulted in my next movie, *Satan's Little Helper.*

Jeff Lieberman • Day Of The Living Me!

October 1999 Big 5-0 party before guests arrived. Me as 'old' and JoAnn as Carmen Miranda

Halloween October 1979. JoAnn as a Vampire and me in mink.

The party crashing Gorilla, my Big five-oh bash

27. A LITTLE HELP FROM SATAN

The inherent creepiness of that moment at my 50th birthday blowout meant that if this was an inspiration for a movie, it would certainly be of the horror variety. I hadn't even toyed with the genre for over twenty years since I made *Just Before Dawn*. The horror genre had evolved tremendously since then with computer generated imagery (CGI) taking the place of practical special effects. With the right amount of money, anything that could be imagined could be put on screen through the use of computer applications.

The 2000's ushered in a period of information overload. The Internet explosion of the late 1990's set the stage for iTunes, iPhones, iPads, YouTube, Netflix, Amazon and video games, all converging into one constant chaotic flow of digital noise. It also coincided with me reaching a point in my creative life where I started feeling a sense of urgency to express my thoughts about modern society without holding back and taking aim at sacred cows whenever possible; the perfect mindset for subversive horror. Surveying the landscape, it struck me how difficult it must be to be a child in these times. How do you process such a bombardment of information when 99 percent of it is pure bullshit? When virtually anyone with a computer, or smart phone and minimum typing skills can spout their opinions in the guise of news, or state flat out lies in the guise of facts to millions of gullible readers and viewers around the world.

If adults can't discern what's true on the Internet, what about a child? And increasingly realistic video games were getting harder and harder to differentiate from live action television. This was the genesis for my next movie, *Satan's Little Helper*, where I reopened the subversive gates in full attack mode. Religion, the innocence of children, the gullibility of the public, everything I could aim at that pissed me off was fashioned into the narrative in some way. And to top it off, I set the movie on that most subversive holiday of the year, Halloween. I worked the narrative in such a way that at one point one of the main characters logically concludes, "Jesus is Satan!" Try spouting that line in any other genre!

I'd been noodling with an idea about a kid writing a letter to Satan just the way kids write dear Santa letters every Christmas, but instead of addressing it to the North Pole, he sends his dear Satan letter to Hell. A kid writing to Santa might ask ole St. Nick for presents, maybe to come to his house for a Christmas eve visit and even offer to be Santa's "little helper" along with his crew of elves. Well, what would a kid ask Satan for? To come and kill somebody for him, what else? So this was the premise I'd been kicking around, but I had no idea who this "Satan" was. I mean how to depict him. I'd never do a movie with a cliché fake Satan character who breathed fire, or morphed into other creatures, or even pretty girls. The very idea of Satan is based on the supernatural, like ghosts and vampires and those things never interested me as I think they're corny and not scary. I thought Linda Blair was scary in The Exorcist until her head started rotating.

What's scary is what's real. For instance, one word, Cancer, is scarier everywhere in the world than any horror movie ever made. So the Satan the little boy called for, or conjured up, had to be a real person for the idea to work for me. No special effects. And he had to be the embodiment of evil, which of course included taking advantage of a naïve little kid.

That led me to the "aha moment" as I combined this idea with the gorilla at my birthday party, and switched it to a Satan costume instead of a gorilla suit. And instead of meeting him at a party, we meet him going around a suburban neighborhood on Halloween killing people and dragging them out of their houses in broad daylight and propping them up as parts of the victim's Halloween lawn displays. Since it's Halloween this all seems normal, just like the Gorilla guy did at my party, so instead of calling the cops people in the neighborhood pose to take a selfie with this maniac and he would also be the Satan the naive kid is on the lookout for.

But the kid needed a reason to be so obsessed with Satan. Sure it's cool that it's Satan instead of Santa Claus because going to the opposite of the cliché automatically gains a certain amount of mileage right there. Just by turning the phrase "Santa's little helper" into *Satan's Little Helper* is an instant attention getter. Oh, goodness, how mischievous! But there still has to be a credible reason the kid's into Satan at such a young age. He needs to

Adventures of a Subversive Cult Filmmaker from the Golden Age.

be obsessed with Satan somehow. Not possessed like Linda Blair's character in *The Exorcist*, but obsessed, because possessed connotes supernatural. Fictional bullshit. Obsessed is a real human emotion and condition. But why?

For the next few days I mulled over every aspect of this question. Maybe his parents are Satanists. Didn't feel right, too contrived, Satanists just happen to be living right smack in the middle of a nice family neighborhood?

Good idea for a sit-com maybe, but not this.

By the way, what I'm talking about is not the idea of the movie, it's the plot. The idea of the movie is showing the embodiment of evil in a novel way, in this case through a costumed psychopath who is mistaken for someone familiar and trusted and welcomed into someone's home with open arms, just like what could have happened at my birthday party had things taken a different turn. But in order for the plot to be a kid so obsessed with Satan that he invites him into his home, there had be a good reason for it.

I was meandering around an airport gate area waiting to board a plane when I noticed child after child, seated with their parents, glued to their handheld video games and virtually oblivious to the world around them. Even when it was time to board they stayed focused on their tiny screens while shuffling ahead in line to the gate. They even made noises to emulate the explosions they were seeing, as if they were in on the game's action themselves.

These kids were obsessed with these things. Obsessed? Could this hook into my idea somehow? The games all had at their core the age-old good guys vs bad guys format – whether they be superhuman characters like Spiderman, Batman or The Flash. What if the main character was a bad guy? What if he was Satan?

If my young character was obsessed with a video game centered around Satan, then the Devil would fulfil the same fantasy role as Spiderman, Superman, Batman, the Hulk or Antman. Among super heroes and super villains, Satan is the baddest super villain of them all. And who's his arch nemesis? Why Jesus of course. I tried to put my RAM mental flow on hold, then turn it back in the time line to my own childhood to see the world of today from a kid's point of view. If Jesus were a character in a video game, he'd just be another super hero with unique powers, like the ability to walk on water, cure lepers, turn water into wine and have a father who just happens to be God. His enemy, Satan, is hell-bent on destroying mankind, or at least turning them away from all things righteous and holy.

Incorporate these two characters into a cartoonish video game then turn the tables and make the bad guy the main character with the player helping him achieve his dastardly deed. And there I had it, *Satan's Little Helper!* The name of the game would also be the name of the movie (somewhat repeating what I did with Remote Control) The kid will be obsessed with this game and all things Satan. He will act out the game in real life like so many kids do while emulating Star Wars battles with light saber duels. And when this kid sees someone dressed as Satan on Halloween, he thinks the man is play-acting his favorite video game when he's actually an insane serial killer.

So when the kid asks, "Can I be your helper?"

The man nods menacingly, knowing he's found the perfect gullible victim to help him wreak havoc on humanity.

The whole thing felt so right to me because it was the essence of subversive filmmaking, way outside social norms and good taste. One hundred percent politically incorrect.

And it allowed me to satirize so many other things along with way, things like religion and contemporary child rearing.

The independent financing came very quickly and we cast the enormously talented Amanda Plummer to play the role of the little boy's mother with the blonde beauty Kathryn Winnick playing his college-age sister. Filming was very complicated as the movie was set in a fictional place I named Bell Island, which was located off the coast of New England. But in fact we did most of the filming in Westchester County New York, using a house in White Plains as a central location; while I depended on movie magic editing techniques, such as intercutting second unit shots of actual coastal New England locations to give the illusion we were actually spending the day with this family in their isolated island community.

During filming the first indications of resistance to the subject matter became apparent when, upon hearing the title of the movie, people refused to allow shooting in or even near their houses. This was not the southern bible belt; this was in a supposedly sophisticated suburb just north of New York City. We actually had to change the working title to 'The Little Helper' to get through the production and when we wrapped, some of the locals who were wise to us posted signs reading "Don't come back!"

As soon as the movie was completed it was invited to the Tribeca Film festival where it was very well received and scored the best reviews of my career in both major trades, *Variety* and *The Hollywood Reporter.*

Adventures of a Subversive Cult Filmmaker from the Golden Age.

From left, Katheryn Winnick, Amanda Plummer and Jeff

Camera operator Doug Pellegrino shooting Satan and his little Helper's shopping cart rampage.

28. THE GROOM REAPER

At the V.I.P. tent at Tribeca I met a young lady named Ali Hart who shared that the Network she worked for, Court TV, was entering the area of scripted programming and looking for factual, crime-based series ideas. I immediately recalled an idea I had some twenty years earlier, which occurred to me while reading about a spousal murder. The article recounted how this couple first met, high school sweethearts and all that. Their romantic courtship and fairy tale wedding resulted in one of them stabbing and then decapitating the other exactly thirty years after their wedding day. Of course they were madly in love when they tied the knot and had no idea they were heading toward such a horrible fate. But after all, that can be said about every spousal murder. So, what if someone at their wedding did know? A mysterious uninvited guest who knows what's going to happen and recounts it all as our narrator while the happy marriage slowly deteriorates into a murderous disaster. That mythical figure only interacts with the television audience. I called him "The Groom Reaper." Ms. Hart loved it and soon I was up at Court TV pitching to their executives. They paid me to write a pilot script and when finished they gave me the green light to look for a host to play The Groom Reaper for the pilot which I would also direct. My first pick was John Waters, a perfect fit for the character. After a short chat on the phone, John asked me to send him the script and he'd read it on his plane ride to LA. He soon called me from the airport to tell me he loved it and that was that, we had a pilot order.

The name of the show? *Til Death Do Us Part* of course, a natural title for the subject matter. Before you go running to look it up, there's sixteen other TV shows and movies with that title. Somehow we were able to be the

Adventures of a Subversive Cult Filmmaker from the Golden Age.

seventeenth. The series ran a full season and was about to get renewed when Court TV was bought up by Time Warner who changed their name and format to Tru-TV which precluded scripted programming. The most fun I got out of the experience was working with Waters, one of the sharpest, hippest totally original characters I've encountered. Some artists consciously invent a persona but I think in John's case he just did what came naturally all his life and his unique persona just grew out of it. I maintain a friendship with him to this day and since I don't believe in anything about Christmas the only thing I look forward to at that time of year is his custom made hilarious Christmas cards.

With John Waters.

Promotional comic book for the series.

29. THE HORROR CIRCUIT

My return to the horror genre led to my being invited to many Horror and sci-fi conventions as well as fantasy film festivals around the world. I'll start with one convention sampling then follow with a selection from a fantasy film festival to give you a taste of this unexpected late in life renaissance I was experiencing.

The horror convention, a gathering of like minded fans of the genre has been around for decades, but by the late '90s it really exploded into the mainstream attracting huge crowds of fans anxious to meet their favorite personalities in person, get their autograph on various items they brought with them and then get a picture with them. All that comes with a price that they eagerly pay. When I was first invited to one of these it all seemed very strange to me. It made me uncomfortable enough just writing my autograph for people, but now I was expected to charge them for it. And even if I wanted to give out autographs for free I couldn't because it would anger the other 'celebrities' who were charging for theirs and even charging extra to have their pictures taken with fans.

The biggest of the horror/sci-fi conventions was the Chiller Theatre Theater Expo held bi-annually at the Hilton Hotel in Parsippany New Jersey. Both the spring and fall additions would attract upwards of twenty thousand fans.

First starting as a strictly horror themed gathering with my childhood TV horror host hero Zacherley as its resident ghoul, Chiller gradually grew to larger venues and a broader appeal. While maintaining the horror name and theme they expanded their net to also include mostly nostalgic celebrity figures from other genres and even just popular TV stars. My celebrity came

Adventures of a Subversive Cult Filmmaker from the Golden Age.

from being the guy who made those movies they grew up with, first saw on TV and then VHS and Blu-ray, forms now referred to as 'physical media.'

The Chiller convention took over the entire Hilton Hotel for the weekend. The huge main ballroom with floor to ceiling windows was reserved for the biggest name celebrities.

Lower echelon shlubs like me were delegated to a series of small windowless rooms with irritating fluorescent lighting and no ventilation. My fellow celebs ranged from Lou "The Hulk" Ferrigno, Linda Blair, Ex Rolling Stone Mick Taylor and five members of Tony Soprano's main crew from The Sopranos. Notorious ice skater Tanya Harding set up shop in the table next to me.

When the doors opened and the crowds started wandering in the temperature, and B.O. level escalated noticeably. My first time doing this I was flabbergasted at the variety of paraphernalia the fans brought for me to sign, stuff I'd never seen before like foreign posters of my movies, figurine merchandise, publicity stills, even original laser discs of my films. I tried my best to answer all their questions while other fans waited patiently in line behind them. It was up to me to cut these conversations short or they'd go on for hours with no regard for those waiting their turns.

To the casual reader, or just the average sane person, signing your name for twenty bucks (it's since been raised to thirty!) might not seem like 'work.' And it's not. At least for the first hour or so. But as the day wears on and the air gets thicker, greeting the next fan with a welcoming smile and hardy handshake actually becomes a chore. So is being careful not to say anything that might offend them, which is probably the hardest part of all of this for me. But there was no denying you sure could accumulate money fast this way and in no time, I piled up a sizable stash, mostly in twenty dollar bills.

Six o'clock came around none too soon and I covered my table and scooted out of there. After sitting all day I needed a workout to stretch and breath myself back to life. Fortunately, the hotel had a huge fully equipped gym.

Lying on the mat to stretch I turned my head to the left and found myself face to face with actress Mariel Hemmingway lying on her back doing stretches on an adjacent mat. No kid anymore she was still gorgeous and aging took nothing away from her earthy grounded quality. But I couldn't recall her being in any horror or sci-fi movie so I asked,

"What brings you to a horror convention? Was there something scary about *Manhattan* I missed?"

She giggled with a big genuine smile. She was definitely not a

Hollywood type and unlike some of the other names at the convention who treated their past glories as if it were the present, she was very self-deprecating about it, and this was actually her first experience doing this. Obviously, *Manhattan* was not the draw and she told me it was for her role in *Superman Four.*

"Four? There was a four?"

"There was but very few people saw it, thank God."

"Oh."

She also told me she was instructed to bring along a bunch of semi nude modeling shots and publicity stills from her movie *Star 80* and lots of nude shots from the resultant Playboy spread that year. That's what the fans will want her to sign, not anything from the PG rated Superman Four. While we proceeded with our workouts, she confided displaying those nudie pictures embarrassed her so with the Playboy pictures she's been signing her name across her breasts. A last ditch attempt at modesty.

Next morning, I headed to the front desk to convert my roll of twenty-dollar bills into as many hundreds as I could. Other savvy celebrity guests were already waiting on line to do the same and among them was Mariel in her workout attire. I asked her if she was heading to the gym and she said she was actually going for a hike in some local park a friend from LA recommended. Didn't seem like there were any hiking parks in this part of New Jersey but hey, if there was one, it sure sounded good to get out into the fresh air before another day in that airless room. When she told me she was hiking it alone I asked if I could join her and she was very receptive to it. In fact she was looking around for someone who said they'd give her lift there and I told her I lived in New York and had driven to the convention so we could take my car.

When I turned onto the main road I asked for directions and she checked her phone for text messages, then found our destination was a park about five miles away. Part of the park contained a steep hill with a hiking trail winding to the top, which is what motivated her to try it.

She entered the park's name into google maps, and soon shouted out 'make a left, make a left!'

She meant to make a left on the road we just passed. How in hell am I supposed to do that?

"You're supposed to tell me BEFORE we get to it!"

"I just saw the sign."

I had to crack up laughing while I found the next available place to make a u-turn. I explained that we'd just met yesterday and we're arguing like an old married couple and that my wife JoAnn does the exact same thing when she navigates from her cell phone.

She took it good naturedly and then focused on her navigating.

So, we get to our destination, park in the lot, then start up the hill with Mariel leading the way. She's taking monster strides and I soon realized this walk in the park wasn't just a walk in the park. But the air was freshened with Pine tree's and a pleasant breeze and that stale aired dungeon convention room seemed like a hundred miles away.

As we ascended, I made some small talk between gasps.

"You realize you just met me at a horror festival? For all you know I could be bullshitting about being one of the guests and am actually some crazed fan and potential serial killer and you're out here in the woods with me all alone?"

She turned and looked at me incredulously, then continued ahead. "What? No way I could be a serial killer. Those are the most dangerous kind!"

I actually took her reaction as sort of a put down. Did I really come off as being that harmless? I mean, I am, but isn't that assumption similar to racial profiling?

We reached the hilltop, which afforded us a pretty nice view of the nearby Jersey Turnpike. As Mariel sucked it all in with a few 'cleansing breaths,' I continued my probably annoying, Woody Allenesque monologue.

"The room I'm doing the signings in has no air and no windows to open. And with all that body odor it's like a gas chamber. At least you're in the main room with lots of windows so if you can't take anymore of the stupid questions they bombard with you can always jump."

"Oh boy, I do get some crazy questions."

"But you're only on the second floor so that wouldn't work. Imagine trying to commit suicide by jumping out a second floor window and only winding up in the hospital with casts on your arms and legs? How embarrassing is that?"

"That would be," she giggled, then led the way for the descent. I asked her if she's heading back to LA when the convention wraps and she said she's going on to some promotion for a documentary she's in.

When we parted ways at the end of the convention we exchanged phone numbers and I told her I'd call her when I'm next in LA.

Once home I recounted my chance meeting and hiking trip with Mariel to JoAnn and she said she just read about a movie or documentary about

Mariel and all the suicides in her family and how she doesn't want to be the next one.

"What?!"

I dashed to my computer and did a search and sure enough, the documentary JoAnn was referring to was done by Barbara Koppel and called *Running from Crazy*, the film Mariel was telling me about that she was going on from the convention to promote. Here's what Google had to say:

"Actress Mariel Hemingway, the granddaughter of author Ernest Hemingway, pursues a better understanding of her family history of suicide and mental illness…" "After seven suicides in the Hemmingway family including her grandfather Ernest and older sister Margaux, Mariel declares war on depression…"

"Oh, shit…"

Sure I knew Ernest Hemmingway blew his brains out with a shotgun but the reason I had no idea death by self ran in the Hemmingway family is I have no interest in the offscreen lives of Hollywood people. Stuff covered feverishly in People Magazine and all those Hollywood gossip shows was another world to me.

So now I'm feeling like a complete jerk, which was far from a novel feeling for me but still, I must've sounded like a real douche bag to Mariel, making jokes about her wanting to jump out a second story window.

As it turned out I was overestimating my douchery because a couple of months later I was in LA and Mariel and I met for lunch in Santa Monica at a very strictly vegan restaurant on Main Street and my first order of business was to apologize for my insensitivity in making light of suicide. Mariel said it didn't bother her in the least, she knew I had no idea about her family history and what she was struggling with and in fact she's been counseled to learn to laugh about it on her road to living a mentally healthy life. And laugh she did so I immediately transformed my guilt into a mitzvah and considered sending her a bill for my therapy.

Speaking of bills, the place she suggested for lunch was not only vegan, it was 'glot' vegan. There was nothing recognizable to me on the menu and since Mariel had been there before I suggested she do the ordering which she did. Soon the waitress – or 'wait-person' since this was LA – arrived with a pitcher of a brown liquid concoction that looked identical to swamp water with little lumpy things floating in it that seemed to be moving. When I poured a glass for Mariel she waved it off.

"I'm not eating. I have a yoga class in a half hour right down the block."

Adventures of a Subversive Cult Filmmaker from the Golden Age.

So after a pleasant chat we air kissed and she scooted off, leaving me staring at the pile of rabbit food and glass of pond ooze before me. I asked for the check without touching any of it.

The second aspect of my (as Variety put it) 'back to his horror roots' period was the several film festivals around the world I was invited to over the following years which focused specifically on the horror and sci fi genres. Unbeknownst to me an organization was formed decades ago called 'The Fantasy Film Festival Federation' or FFFF with member groups in Brussels, Ravenna Italy, Amsterdam, Copenhagen, Helsinki, Hamburg, Edinburgh Scotland, Toronto Canada, Porto Alegre, Brazil, you name it and over the ensuing years I was invited to pretty much all of them.

Night Visions festival party in my honor, American Embassy, Helsinki, Finland

Crashing Tippi Hedren's autograph table, New Jersey horror convention

Attempting to get my assistant drunk. Frightmare in the Falls horror convention.

With friend and fellow Horror Meister Mick Garris

Music Box Theater marquee, Chicago Illinois

Adventures of a Subversive Cult Filmmaker from the Golden Age.

Dedicated fan, Cinema Wasteland convention, Cleveland

Coffin signing, Niagara Falls convention

Betsy Palmer, Cinemawasteland convention, Cleveland Ohio

30. DON'T BREAK ANYTHING!

One festival in particular stood out, when I was invited to serve as "El Presidente" of the jury at The Fantastic Film Festival of the University of Malaga in Malaga Spain. JoAnn accompanied me to the seaside city of Malaga located on the southern most tip of Spain, not far from the Rock of Gibraltar. From the moment we arrived the festival hosts treated us like royalty, putting us up in a top shelf traditional old hotel for the entire ten days of the festival.

I didn't realize that the guest of honor was Tippi Hedren, until we did the press introductions and I was asked to pose next to her. My icebreaker with Tippi was connecting my movie *Squirm* with her *The Birds*, using the phrase 'the early bird gets the worm' for the connection. Lame I know, but it was good enough to get us started because there was an instant positive chemistry between us that I can't explain. Maybe one of those past lives things.

Her fiancé, renowned veterinarian Martin Dinnes was beyond fascinating to talk to. Or rather listen to because nothing I could say could top hearing about his caring for an assortment of wild animals which included killer whales and elephants, along with exotic animals wealthy people buy illegally and then tire of and neglect. Some of Martin's clients included Mike Tyson and his Bengal tigers and Michael Jackson and his menagerie of creatures which included his pet Chimpanzee.

For the next few days the four of us were inseparable, drinks at the hotel followed by dinner out, then breakfast somewhere the following mornings.

At a restaurant for lunch one day, Tippi suddenly glanced around at the surroundings and said the place looked familiar to her. That her son-in-law Antonio might own the building. That seemed really strange to me as we were Americans in the southernmost tip of Spain. Clueless, I asked, "Who's Antonio?"

"Antonio Banderes. Melanie's husband."

"Oh, Melanie Griffen. That's right, she's your daughter. Didn't realize they were married."

Once again my lack of *People Magazine* knowledge reared its ugly head.

"So, why would he own this place?"

"He was born here and grew up in this town. He and Melanie still keep a beach house here in Marbella, right on the water. A yacht too."

Just then the manager of the restaurant recognized Tippi and rushed over. Turns out Antonio did own the building. Normally this would've instantly registered to me that this meal would definitely be on the house but alas, we weren't paying anyway because everything was on the festival.

When the manager finished gushing over Tippi I pulled a Cubano cigar from my top pocket and leaned back on my chair.

"So, lemmme get this straight. They have a yacht parked at a beach house nobody's using."

Tippi nodded as she took another sip of white wine.

"Okay, here's what I'm picturing. Me sitting on the rear deck of the yacht with a Cubano in one hand and a martini in the other watching the sunset over the Mediterranean. Can you make that happen?"

"Well, I can certainly try."

With that, Tippi pulled out her cell phone, got up and headed to a quiet corner of the restaurant. As the waiter served up bowls of the house specialty garlic soup, I could tell that Martin was really enjoying all of this. Guess he had an affinity for pushy New Yorkers with a minimum of social graces.

When Tippi returned she sat back down and savored a whiff of her garlic soup.

"Smells divine."

"What'd she say?"

"They're in Mexico. They have a house there."

"They live in Mexico?"

"No, their main house is in Hancock Park but they have one in Mexico too. She said it's fine but don't break anything."

"Cool!"

The festival arranged for a Mercedes van and driver to take us out to Los

Jeff Lieberman • Day Of The Living Me!

Monteros, just outside of Marbella and around a forty minute drive from our hotel. Another guest of the festival, actor Michael Ironside joined us with his wife and 12-year-old daughter expanding our group to three couples and a child.

After exploring the holy caves of Los Monteros we headed on to Marbella but when we exited the freeway and came to a stop, another car plowed into us from behind, sending all our belongings to the back of the van. Fortunately, we were all wearing seatbelts, and nobody was hurt but this delay was surely going to screw up my appointment with Antonio's boat. As gazed at the position of the setting late afternoon sun, I just couldn't believe this once in a lifetime opportunity could be ruined by some asshole driver who was probably texting while driving.

By the time we arrived at the Banderas house the sun had already set, but it was certainly still light enough to see that what Tippi referred to as a 'beach house' was actually a full out, century old waterfront Spanish mansion complete with pool, guest quarters and a thatched tiki like outdoor lounging and entertaining area which was much closer to what I would refer to as a beach house.

Martin had ordered a case of wine in advance of our arrival so we were all sloshed in no time.

I wandered from the group to explore the house and came across Antonio's office den where my attention was drawn to the actual Zorro costume he wore in the movie. Cool! It was mounted on a display form and the sword was setting in its gilded sheath. I pulled out the sword, then headed out across the expansive living room, past an array of statuary and valuable antiques, then up a white marble curving staircase to the second level. Once there I turned around and broke into my Zorro imitation. But not Antonio's Zorro, Guy Williams' version from the old black and white TV series of my youth. I held out my sword and declared to all: 'I am Zorro! Sargent Garcia, prepare to die!'

I started swinging the sword in a dueling motion while I descended the stairs. Then Tippi came rushing into the living room frantically waving her arms.

"No! Remember what Melanie said, don't break anything!"

Over the course of that festival in Malaga JoAnn and I met and partied with dozens of thirty something's and the more wine we consumed the more we offered open invitations to come visit us in New York. We told them we were 'empty nesters' and had a nice big house in Westchester just north of the city. We'd exchange phone numbers and they'd hand me their cards, scribbling details on the back.

Adventures of a Subversive Cult Filmmaker from the Golden Age.

One of these empty nest invitees was a very bright, very artsy, 30ish, Catalan videographer named Jordi who returned the favor with an invite to his own nest for dinner. We accepted and when we arrived at his address we weren't surprised to see that he lived in an equally artsy building, an old factory conversion, the typical type of long abandoned buildings that attract artists to transform them into cheap living spaces.

We entered a large loft expanse where Jordi had all his computer editing equipment set up, along with an array of video cameras and lights.

Jordi introduced us to his girlfriend who had prepared a wonderful dinner and as the night went on, I did a video of this whacky Spaniard presenting his wine parings and the story behind each of his selections. Then nature called and I excused myself and headed to the bathroom we passed on the way into the loft. Jordi and his girlfriend suddenly objected. "No,no, no. Don't use that one, use the one upstairs!"

That seemed odd to me because the one upstairs was located right off their sleeping loft bedroom so one would think that would be the one they wouldn't want guests to use. But it was their place so I complied.

Why am I telling you all this? Well, when the festival was over, we took a short flight to Barcelona, then boarded a connecting flight back to New York. Right after we took off I found myself having trouble getting comfortable because the stack of business sized cards given me by all those fans was pushing against my hip. I pulled out the cards, took the rubber band off and started flipping through them. There were over fifty cards with names and phone numbers of all those thirty something fans, none of whom I remembered anything about. I turned to JoAnn,

"How many of these people did we invite to our house?"

JoAnn thought about it, then shrugged, "Pretty much all of them."

I pondered the implications of that. "These are all horror fans. We don't know anything about any of them but we invited all of them to come stay with us."

Flipping through the cards, I stopped at Jordi's which triggered a dreadful thought.

"Do you remember at Jordi's when I needed to use the bathroom and they stopped me from using the one right nearby on the main floor? Wasn't that weird?"

"Come to think of it I did think that was odd."

"Only thing we know about him is he's a horror fan who does videos and is a fan of my stuff. For all we know he didn't want me going to the main floor bathroom because he had three bodies hanging on meat hooks over the tub."

Then I went silent. JoAnn looked at me. She'd seen this face many times before.

"You're gonna write another movie aren't you?"

She was right. And when we got home I dropped my luggage, dashed to my desk and fired up my computer. Then I noticed that my chair seemed very low. Either someone had broken in while we were away and instead of ransacking the house decided to lower my office chair, or my old age shrinking process had accelerated! I raised the chair a couple of notches then heatedly pounded out the title of the movie idea that hit me on the plane, 'CINEMUERTE' . . .

With Tippi Hedron

Tippi, me and JoAnn

31. REGRETS?

Like Paul Anka, I've had a few. Actually, more than a few, but lemme mention just one because it's a whopper. In fact I realized I subconsciously skipped over it while chronicling events that occurred during that period just after my first film The Ringer was garnering so much unexpected attention. A painful memory of a moment in time that's etched in my memory like it happened just yesterday.

Back to 1972. (one last time, I promise!) Jerry Berger at King Features showed The Ringer to some friends, among them a talent manager named Buddy Morra who was really impressed and wanted to meet me as a potential client. Jerry connected us and soon after I trekked up to the offices of Rollins and Joffe on Central Park South.

I'd never heard of the company's principals Jack Rollins and Charles Joffe so I had no idea they were the most prestigious personal managers in all of show business at that time.

I met with Buddy at his outer desk. He said his main job was to discover and develop new talent and used as an example one named Robert Klein who was pioneering performing concerts at colleges, (which would later be known as playing the 'college circuit.')

In no time Buddy and I were joking with each other and he eagerly set up another meeting to screen The Ringer to one of his bosses, Charles Joffe at a screening room of a talent agency called International Creative Management, or ICM. To me the word agency was synonymous with advertising so it struck me as funny that they were selling human talent instead of cornflakes.

Charlie Joffe met us at the ICM screening room which, unlike the lavish theater-like facilities of today's agencies, was just a small conference room equipped with a projector. They held up the screening until a man named Sam Cohen was able to pull himself away from his desk and duck in to watch the film.

So there we were, me, Buddy, Charlie and Sam Cohen and some young geek who knew how to thread up a 16mm projector which made way too much noise, coupled with the fact that the only sound was coming from the tinny speakers mounted on either side.

When the film was over, Charlie and Sam shook my hand and seemed impressed, then Sam invited us to his office when we finished talking.

Charlie took a moment with me and said these words,

"You're very clever. But if you want to make movies you've got to do more than clever. Only one person can get away with clever for ninety minutes and that's Woody."

"Woody Allen?"

"We manage him. Jack and I produced Take the Money and Bananas."

Holy shit. I loved those movies!

Instead of just praising my little film and leaving it at that, Charlie shined a light on a simple truth about it, which I took as devastating criticism of me. Like I was being found out. Exposed as some kind of con man. What everyone liked so much about the Ringer was this thing Charlie was referring to as clever and in sizing up my talent and potential he recognized my ability to use my wit to sustain variations of one central joke for 20 minutes. But to do a real movie you can't just rely on that. You need a real story with real characters and if anything, the experience of writing Blade with Ernie Pintoff didn't display any of those abilities. In fact, Blade wasn't even clever. Charlie's intention was not to shake my confidence. He was talking from the perspective of a talent manager who can focus in on strengths to develop as an artist. But all I heard was Woody Allen. I was no Woody Allen and was nowhere near ready for this. What in hell was I doing there? I wanted to flee but instead was herded into Sam Cohen's office, which was lined wall to wall with more autographed pictures of famous movie stars than on the walls of the Carnegie Deli. Only Sam was in the pictures with them because they were all his clients. Woody Allen, Robert Altman, E.L. Doctorow, Nora Ephron, Bob Fosse, Jackie Gleason, Arthur Miller, Paul Newman, Mike Nichols, Arthur Penn, Vanessa Redgrave, Susan Sarandon, Meryl Streep, Lily Tomlin, Kathleen Turner, Sigourney Weaver and Dianne Wiest! Sam Cohen was the freaking head of ICM and the most powerful agent in show business at that time!

Adventures of a Subversive Cult Filmmaker from the Golden Age.

I felt like some schmuck on one of those NBC tours, an outsider looking in on the world of show business. I sunk down in my chair and just listened as Sam and Charlie discussed The Ringer, with Charlie once again bringing up the clever thing, which to me sounded like the word 'sucks' at this point. Sam sat back in his chair, folded his hands in front of him and leveled his glance on me.

"So, what do want to do? What are your goals as a director?" I could've said to be the next Stanly Kubrick. But completely devoid of confidence, instead I muttered,

"I don't really have any. I'm not even sure I want to do this…"

All the air let out of the room. They all exchanged glances. Charlie probably instantly regretted wasting Sam's time as well as his own and Buddy Morro just sat there, head tilted back and eyes closed.

Ten minutes later I was out on 57th street with the film can of the The Ringer tucked under my arm and feeling like I just got hit by a bus.

I'm sure you've heard this hypothetical question countless times, 'if you had it to do over again, what would you do?' The cold truth is you would do the exact same thing you did for the exact same reasons. In order to do otherwise you'd have to possess 20-20 hindsight, which would mean you'd be someone else and not you. It's easy to fantasize me boldly extolling my big dreams and ambitions to Sam Cohen that day but those words really belonged to someone like Steven Spielberg or Martin Scorsese, guys who were obsessed with movie making as kids, who made home movies with their friends and spent countless hours in movie theaters absorbing the works of the great filmmakers around the world. That was never me.

By proceeding without any plan, no defined goal other than to stay afloat, I found my confidence in focusing mainly on my own original ideas which over the course of time, combined with that clever thing Charlie Joffe saw in me, eventually defined who I was through my body of work, my own signature, my voice, however minor or inconsequential it might be in the grand scheme of things. I was right in thinking that I'm no Woody Allen. Nor John Carpenter, or George Romero for that matter. But then again, they're not me. And me at that time really wasn't sure I wanted to make movies as a lifetime career which is why I said what I said at that crucial moment in time.

So you're probably thinking, that doesn't sound like a regret at all. And you're right. But it's not what I said that I regret, it's what I didn't say, which was to tell them what I really DID want to do. Stand-up comedy!

And later on when I learned that aside from managing established people like Woody, Dick Cavett and Robert Klein at the time I met with them, Rollins and Joffe were also shepherding the careers of a bunch of up and coming unknown young comics like David Letterman, Robin Williams, Billy Crystal, Martin Short and many others. Had I just leveled with them and said I wanted to work in the vein of Woody Allen, and focus that clever thing into my own brand of stand-up comedy, who knows how they would've responded. Alas, as with all major regrets, I'll never know what would've happened, but I was able to channel lots of my comedic stylings into my work anyway and critics always made mention of my comedic touch in different ways like 'quirky humor' 'black humor' along with that C word, clever.

My returning to my horror roots in the 2Ks spawned dozens of personal appearances which suddenly put me before festival audiences of as many as 900 people per screening. After one particular showing of *Blue Sunshine*, there I was alone on stage for the question and answer session with microphone in hand and I started to recount the LSD flashback story I told you about, my believing JoAnn was about to give birth to a giant bird. Suddenly I felt a strange energy force. It was as if the spirit of George Burns took hold of me - which was very possible because after all he was God - and I started pacing the stage, sharing that nightmarish child birthing experience with the audience as if it happened yesterday, just like George would. And the audience responded with a burst of laughter that got louder and louder until I wrapped it up to thunderous applause.

So, as fate would have it that's what it took to finally get me to do comedy in front of an audience; present it in the form of stories about my career, those very stories you read (or skimmed through) in this book.

And with each succeeding festival or special screening I sharpened my act, mic in hand, pacing the stages of landmark theaters like The Music Box in Chicago, the New Beverly and Egyptian Theaters in Hollywood, the Cinematheque in Toulouse France and the historic Filmhouse in Edinburgh Scotland. Gradually I started working in stories that were not film related, stories about being a baby boomer born at the perfect place and time to be a first-hand witness to iconic events like being a Polio Pioneer, cutting school to see the Beatles first arrival at Kennedy Airport, attending the first Earth day festival, watching the moon landing on TV, marching in the first Woman's lib parade down fifth avenue, then again in the March on Washington and many others, always sticking to George Burns' credo of making it seem like I was recounting these comedic antidotes for the very first time.

Adventures of a Subversive Cult Filmmaker from the Golden Age.

Okay, so there you have it, a reveal of my biggest regret in life...not grabbing for that golden opportunity to have the top comedy managers in the business help me set out on a career as a stand-up comic. But ponder this, had I taken that path, the world would've had to exist without *Squirm*!

The End

The Author

Special Thanks

JoAnn Lieberman

Joe Toplyn

Jon Tolson

Jeff Rosen

Don Kilcoyne

Fred Berner

Daniel Lieberman